THE AUTOMATIC MILLIONAIRE

A POWERFUL ONE-STEP PLAN TO LIVE
— AND FINISH RICH —

Do It
Once—
The Rest Is
AUTOMATIC!

DAVID BACH

NEW YORK TIMES BESTSELLING AUTHOR OF
Start Late, Finish Rich **AND** *Smart Couples Finish Rich*

PRAISE FOR *The Automatic Millionaire*

"*The Automatic Millionaire* is an automatic winner. David Bach really cares about you: on every page you can hear him cheering you on to financial fitness. No matter who you are or what your income is, you can benefit from this easy-to-apply program. Do it now. You and your loved ones deserve big bucks!"

—Ken Blanchard, coauthor of
The One Minute Manager®

"*The Automatic Millionaire* gives you, step by step, everything you need to secure your financial future. When you do it David Bach's way, failure is not an option."

—Jean Chatzky, Financial Editor, NBC's *Today*

"David Bach's no-spin financial advice is beautiful because it's so simple. If becoming self-sufficient is important to you, then this book is a must."

—Bill O'Reilly, anchor, Fox News, and author of
The O'Reilly Factor and *The No Spin Zone*

"Finally, a book that helps you stop sweating it when it comes to your money! *The Automatic Millionaire* is a fast, easy read that gets you to take action. David Bach is the money coach to trust year in and year out to motivate you financially."

—Richard Carlson, author of
Don't Sweat the Small Stuff

"*The Automatic Millionaire* proves that you don't have to make a lot of money or have a complicated financial plan to get started—you can literally start toward your financial dreams today, in a matter of hours, with just one life-changing secret: Pay yourself first and make it automatic! Equally important, this book shows you how to simplify and automate your entire financial life."

—Harry S. Dent, Jr., investment strategist and
author of *The Roaring 2000s*

"*The Automatic Millionaire* is, simply put . . . a great little book! You can read it in a matter of hours and take action immediately on a powerful, simple, totally AUTOMATIC plan to become a millionaire."

—Robert G. Allen, coauthor of
The One Minute Millionaire

"David Bach makes understanding your finances easy, fun, and exciting. *The Automatic Millionaire* is a practical and smart guide to mastering your relationship with money."

—Barbara De Angelis, Ph.D., author of
What Women Want Men to Know

"More people will become millionaires in the years ahead than in all the previous years of human history. It has never been more possible for you to get out of debt, achieve financial independence, and build a financial fortress around yourself than it is today. This fast-moving book by David Bach gives you the practical strategies and techniques you need to take complete control of your financial life and become the millionaire you want to be."

—Brian Tracy, author of *Goals!*

"David Bach lets you in on the secret to finishing rich, and it's so simple anyone can do it. Read this book, follow his advice, and it will change your life."

—Candace Bahr and Ginita Wall, cofounders of the
Women's Institute for Financial Education (WIFE.org)

"Pay yourself first. It's simple ideas like this that can make all the difference in your financial future. Ignore David Bach's new book at your own peril."

—Al Ries, author of
Focus, the Future of Your Company Depends on It

Turn to page 240 to read about David Bach's new book, coming soon!

Also by David Bach

Start Late, Finish Rich

The Automatic Millionaire Workbook

The Finish Rich Workbook

Smart Couples Finish Rich®

Smart Women Finish Rich®

1001 Financial Words You Need to Know

THE
AUTOMATIC
MILLIONAIRE®

*A Powerful One-Step Plan
to Live and Finish Rich*

DAVID BACH

BROADWAY BOOKS　New York

BROADWAY

A hardcover edition of this book was originally published in 2004 by Broadway Books.

THE AUTOMATIC MILLIONAIRE. Copyright © 2004 by David Bach. All rights reserved. No part of this book may be reproduced or transmitted in any form or by any means, electronic or mechanical, including photocopying, recording, or by any information storage and retrieval system, without written permission from the publisher. For information, address Broadway Books, a division of Random House, Inc.

The Automatic Millionaire, The Latte Factor, DOLP, Smart Women Finish Rich, Smart Couples Finish Rich are registered trademarks of FinishRich, Inc.

PRINTED IN THE UNITED STATES OF AMERICA

BROADWAY BOOKS and its logo, a letter B bisected on the diagonal, are trademarks of Random House, Inc.

This book is designed to provide accurate and authoritative information on the subject of personal finances. While all of the stories and anecdotes described in the book are based on true experiences, most of the names are pseudonyms, and some situations have been changed slightly for educational purposes and to protect each individual's privacy. It is sold with the understanding that neither the Author nor the Publisher is engaged in rendering legal, accounting, or other professional services by publishing this book. As each individual situation is unique, questions relevant to personal finances and specific to the individual should be addressed to an appropriate professional to ensure that the situation has been evaluated carefully and appropriately. The Author and Publisher specifically disclaim any liability, loss, or risk which is incurred as a consequence, directly or indirectly, of the use and application of any of the contents of this work.

Visit our website at www.broadwaybooks.com.

Book design by Bonni Leon-Berman

The Library of Congress has cataloged the hardcover edition as follows:

Bach, David.
    The automatic millionaire : a powerful one-step plan
to live and finish rich / David Bach.
        p. cm.
        (alk. paper)
    1. Finance, Personal. 2. Financial security. I. Title.
HG179.B234 2004
332.024'01—dc21

                                    2003051802

ISBN 0-7679-2382-0

20 19 18

To my English teacher,

Peter Annas.

Thanks for caring and for inspiring me to write.

You changed my life.

CONTENTS

PREFACE TO THE
PAPERBACK EDITION

Thank you for picking up a copy of this new edition of *The Automatic Millionaire* and congratulations on making the choice to create an easier financial future for yourself and your family.

When I originally wrote this book back in 2003, I had a really simple goal: I wanted to help 10 million people achieve financial freedom by showing them how, over the course of their lifetimes, they could become "automatic millionaires."

I knew this goal was a challenging one—but it was also exciting, and I believed it was worth trying for. What I didn't realize when I first started was the power of word of mouth.

As this book reached real people who were looking for real advice, it quickly began to make a real difference in countless lives. As a result, readers began sharing it with their friends, family, and coworkers, and, in no time, at all, this little book exploded around the world. Within a matter of weeks *The Automatic Millionaire* had reached the #1 spot on nearly every bestseller list in America, including those of the *New York Times,* the *Wall Street Journal, USA Today,* and *BusinessWeek.*

Over the next few months, I had the privilege of sharing the *Automatic Millionaire* philosophy on *The Oprah Winfrey Show,* NBC's *Today* show, CBS's *Early Show,* CNN's *American Morning,* and many other television programs.

In less than a year, more than a million copies of *The Automatic Millionaire* were in print and it had been translated into fifteen languages. *BusinessWeek* listed it as the #1 business book of 2004.

The success of this little book has not only been exciting and humbling for me, it's also been educational. I've seen firsthand how great a need there is for simple, actionable coaching on money matters. More important, I've seen how these simple ideas can change people's lives. Indeed, tens of thousands of you have written to me to share the success you are now enjoying as a result of using the tools this book provides.

In this revised paperback edition, I've added a new chapter that highlights some of the success stories we've received. These stories come from real people like you who wanted to get real results—and now are. There are many more of these stories on our web site at **www.finishrich.com.** Don't take my word for it that this stuff works. Read these real-life accounts—and let the real people featured in them encourage you that "if they can do it—you can do it." *The fact is, you can!*

To help readers tailor this book's plan to their own finances and track their progress, I've also written *The Automatic Millionaire Workbook,* which is now available in stores. As a gift to you, I've posted a few chapters of the workbook on our web site for free downloading—along with new tools that I've created to help make your journey to becoming an Automatic Millionaire as simple and easy as possible.

Again, thank you from the bottom of my heart for allow-ing me the opportunity to be your coach. Enjoy the journey this book takes you on—and have fun with it. You deserve to live and finish rich—and I know you can.

David Bach
October 2005

NEW FREE GIFT!
THE AUTOMATIC MILLIONAIRE SEMINAR

I'm so proud of you for reading this book that I want to give you another free gift. On the *Automatic Millionaire* web site at **www.finishrich.com**, you'll find an audio of one of my Automatic Millionaire Seminars, recorded in front of a live audience of 7,000 people. You can download it or listen to the seminar online. Have fun listening!

INTRODUCTION

What if I told you that in just an hour or two I could share with you a system that would slowly but surely transform you into a millionaire?

What if I told you it was a proven system that you could set up in just an hour or two that would require no budget, no discipline, less than ten dollars a day of investment, and could be done over the phone, from the comfort of your home?

What if I told you this system is called The Automatic Millionaire® and that if you spent just an hour or two with me, you could become one? What if I told you it was easy—so easy in fact that once you set it up you'd never have to spend more than ten minutes a month monitoring it?

Would I have your attention? Would you spend an hour or two with me? Would you like to become an Automatic Millionaire?

—DAVID BACH

> If the lines above got your attention—and I hope they did—then please keep reading. If you're in a bookstore, stay where you are and read just a few more pages. I promise that you'll be hooked. This book is designed to be read in just an hour or two and acted on immediately. It's an easy read. It's an easy system. It can help you if you let it because it's based on commonsense financial advice that is tried and true.

WHO STOLE THE AMERICAN DREAM?

Somewhere, somehow, over the last few years, something happened to the American Dream of owning a home in a nice neighborhood, driving a nice car, providing your children (if you have any) with a life better than you had, and retiring with enough money to do what you want to do when you want to do it. What happened is that this dream disappeared for many Americans.

As a result of the shrinking stock market, many Americans have seen their personal wealth evaporate. Between Wall Street's March 2000 peak and the summer of 2002, U.S. stock market losses totaled a whopping $6.9 trillion. As a result, millions of people have been forced out of retirement and back into the work force. How long these people will have to keep working is anyone's guess. At the same time, millions more who had plans to retire in the next five to ten years are wondering, "What just happened? Will I ever retire? Where's my piece of the dream?"

For most Americans, the old approach to investing for the future is simply not working. Consider this: According to the American Savings Education Council, nearly half of all American workers have less than $25,000 in savings—and nearly 60 million Americans (that's one in five) have nothing in the bank. That's right: zero, zilch, nada. At the same time, the latest statistics tell us that the average American currently owes more than $8,400 in credit card debt.

Even the supposedly wealthy baby boom generation is on

shaky financial ground. Roughly 70 million baby boomers will be reaching retirement age over the next fifteen years, yet according to a study by the American Association of Retired Persons, the "typical boomer" has only $1,000 worth of financial assets. We might call them boomers, but their finances are busting.

HOW ARE YOUR FINANCES DOING?

Are you still living paycheck to paycheck? Or is it worse? Are you living paycheck to paycheck and running up so much credit card debt that you can barely manage to pay the monthly minimums? Did you know that if you owe $2,000 in credit card debt and are making just the minimum monthly payments, it will take you more than eighteen years—and a total of more than $4,600—to pay off your balance?

The point of these facts and figures is not to depress you. It's to reassure you that if you're not yet as rich as you want or need to be, you've got lots of company.

If you've read any of my other books—*Start Late, Finish Rich, Smart Women Finish Rich®, Smart Couples Finish Rich®,* or *The Finish Rich Workbook*—you know I have a no-nonsense approach to learning about money. You also know that I've been successful at helping millions of people take action to transform their financial lives by making the subject of money fun and simple. And in that no-nonsense spirit, let me explain what led me to write this book. It's actually very simple.

I THINK YOU DESERVE TO LIVE
THE AMERICAN DREAM . . .

you just need to learn the secret of how to do it!

I decided to write this book because after all of my other books, radio and television appearances, and the hundreds of speeches and seminars I do, people still ask me every single day, "David, what's the secret to getting rich? Is it still possible for me to get rich? Did I miss the boat?"

Even my own friends ask me this. They say things like "David, I don't want to have to meet with an advisor, read a long book, take a class. Just tell me what to do. What's the secret?"

And you know what? There *is* a secret to getting rich in America. And it's a very simple one. In fact, it's so simple that almost no one does it.

It's not only simple; it's also kind of obvious—so obvious that chances are you already know most of it. But that doesn't mean there's nothing for you to learn here. After all, if you don't happen to be rich—and the fact that you're still reading this book means you're probably not—then it doesn't matter that you may already have heard of some of the techniques I'm going to share with you.

Why?

Because it's more than likely you are not using them. And, chances are, neither are your friends. In fact, most Americans are not using these secrets because they are not taught in school the way they should be.

WHAT YOU SHOULD HAVE BEEN TAUGHT IN SCHOOL . . . BUT WEREN'T

The purpose of this book is not just to share the secrets with you. It's also to get you to put them into practice.

Now, let's be clear about something. I'm not promising to "transform your financial situation overnight." This is not a "no money down," place-tiny-little-ads-in-newspapers, buy-our-software-and-newsletter-and-you-too-can-get-rich-instantly book.

And while the title of this book is no exaggeration, I'm not talking about helping you become a millionaire in a few weeks, a few months, or even a few years. What you'll learn is how to become a millionaire—steadily and surely—over the course of your working life. It's the tortoise's approach to wealth, not the hare's. This may not sound as exciting as becoming a millionaire in a couple of weeks or months, but—I promise you—it's a lot more real. Like I said before, it's a tried-and-true, commonsense approach to becoming financially independent—and achieving the American Dream.

Think about how few people get to retire these days with all their debts and obligations behind them, with enough money saved up to live the kind of life they've always dreamed of, still young enough to enjoy it all. Wouldn't you like to be one of these people? Don't you think you deserve to live the American Dream? That's what this little book can do for you.

HOW THIS BOOK WORKS

First, you're going to meet the original Automatic Millionaires. In my years as a financial advisor, author, and speaker, I've actually met hundreds of Automatic Millionaires. What's amazing is that they are all around you and you'd never know it. Jim and Sue McIntyre, whose story you're going to hear in the first chapter, were the first I met, and what I learned from them changed my life.

So read their story and let it sink in. It contains a powerful message that can change your thinking about money right now. And once your thinking has changed, it will be easy to change your actions. After that, the following seven chapters will lay out exactly what you need to do to follow in their footsteps and become an Automatic Millionaire yourself.

TAKING THE COMPLEX WORLD OF MONEY AND MAKING IT SIMPLE

There are thousands and thousands of books about money. They all promise to teach you how to get rich. Chances are, you already own some of these books. Chances are, you bought them with good intentions but either never read them or, worse, tried to read them but found they confused you or put you to sleep.

This book won't confuse you and it won't put you to sleep. It is simple and straightforward, and in just a few hours it will teach you everything you need to know to become an Automatic Millionaire.

The philosophy behind The Automatic Millionaire®:
- You don't have to make a lot of money to be rich.
- You don't need discipline.
- You don't need to be "your own boss." (Yes, you can still get rich being an employee.)
- By using what I call The Latte Factor®, you can build a fortune on a few dollars a day.
- The rich get rich (and stay that way) because they pay themselves first.
- Homeowners get rich; renters get poor.
- *Above all, you need an "automatic system" so you can't fail.*

YOU WILL LEARN HOW TO MAKE YOUR PLAN AUTOMATIC

What it all boils down to is this:

If your financial plan is not automatic, you will fail! An investment plan that requires you to be disciplined and stick to a budget and write checks manually every couple of weeks simply will not work. You have a busy life. You don't have time to sit down every few weeks and figure out how to save and whom to send checks to. Haven't you already tried to budget and save? It's not working, is it? Yet this is what most Americans are trying to do. It is a recipe for frustration and failure.

There is, however, a simple solution.

The one way to create lasting financial change that will help you build real wealth over time is to . . .

MAKE YOUR FINANCIAL PLAN AUTOMATIC!

Making your financial plan automatic is the one step that virtually guarantees that you won't fail financially. Why? Because by making it automatic, you will have set yourself up for success. And as you will learn in this little book, you can do this in literally minutes.

That's why this book is subtitled "*A Powerful One-Step Plan to Live and Finish Rich.*" The one step is making all aspects of your finances AUTOMATIC!

What do I mean by a plan that is automatic? I mean a plan that, once you've set it up, allows you to go about your life and not spend a lot of time thinking—or, worse, worrying—about your money. You know why this matters? Because ultimately what is missing in our lives today . . . *is a life*! Make your financial plan automatic and one of the most powerful things you will get out of it is worry-free time—which ultimately means getting back more of your life.

If the idea of becoming an Automatic Millionaire with a simple, totally automated plan appeals to you, then you have come to the right place. Don't worry if right now it sounds too simple. As you'll see in the next few hours, because of its unbelievably simple approach, this is an unbelievably easy book to get through. What's more, each chapter ends with a short summary outline I call **Automatic Millionaire Action**

Steps, which makes crystal clear exactly what you can do today to start yourself on the road to accumulating real wealth . . . automatically.

It really can be done. As you'll see, if Jim and Sue McIntyre could become Automatic Millionaires, anyone can. Including you. So let's get started. In just a few hours, I think you'll be pleasantly surprised by how much your thinking has changed—and how ready to take action you are.

FREE! AUTOMATIC MILLIONAIRE AUDIO

As one more way to say thank you for reading this book, I'd like to offer you a new audio program I've developed. It's called:

The Automatic Millionaire Jumpstart

I created it as a bonus to help you really become inspired to take action immediately on what you learn in this book. Please visit my web site at www.finishrich.com or go directly to www.finishrich.com/automaticmillionaire. You'll hear an audio interview with additional insights. Enjoy!

CHAPTER ONE

MEETING THE AUTOMATIC MILLIONAIRE

I'll never forget when I met my first Automatic Millionaire. I was in my mid-twenties and was teaching an investment class at a local adult-education program. Jim McIntyre, a middle-aged middle manager for a local utility company, was one of my students. He and I hadn't spoken much until one day when he came up after class to ask if he could make an appointment with me to review his and his wife's financial situation.

The request surprised me. Though I felt strongly (and still do) that just about everyone can benefit from the advice of a qualified financial planner, Jim didn't strike me as the type who would seek it out.

I told him I'd be happy to set up a meeting, but if he wanted my help, his wife would have to come too, as my group managed money only for couples who worked on their finances together.

Jim smiled. "No problem," he said. "Sue's the reason I'm here. She took your *Smart Women Finish Rich* seminar and told me I should sign up for your course. I've liked what you've had to say, and we both figure it's time to do some financial planning. You see, I'm planning to retire next month."

Now I was really surprised. I didn't say anything, but as I looked Jim up and down, I doubted he could be in a position to retire. From the few comments he had made in class, I knew he was in his early fifties and had worked for the same company for thirty years, never earning much more than $40,000 a year, and didn't believe in budgets. I also knew that he considered himself to be "ultraconservative," so I figured he couldn't have made a fortune in the stock market.

My Grandma Rose Bach had taught me never to judge a book by its cover. But something didn't add up. Maybe Jim had just inherited a lot of money. For his sake, I hoped so.

"WHAT AM I MISSING HERE?"

When the McIntyres came into my office a few days later, they looked exactly like what they were: hardworking, "average Joe" Americans. What has stuck in my mind about Jim is that he was wearing a short-sleeved dress shirt with a plastic pocket protector in his breast pocket. His wife, Sue, had a little more flair, with some seriously blond highlights. She was a beautician, a couple of years younger than Jim.

The thing was, they didn't act like middle-aged people. They were holding hands like two high school kids on a first date, bubbling with excitement. Before I could ask how I could help them, Jim started talking about his plans and what he would do with his free time. As he did, Sue kept exclaiming, "Isn't it great he can retire so young! Most people can't retire until they reach sixty-five if then, and here's Jim able to do it at fifty-two!"

"LET'S NOT GET AHEAD OF OURSELVES."

After ten minutes of this, I had to interrupt. "Guys, your enthusiasm is contagious, but let's not get ahead of ourselves here. I've met with literally hundreds of potential retirees over the last few years, and I have to tell you—hardly any of them have been able to retire in their early fifties." I looked Jim in the eye. "Usually people come to my office to find out *if* they can retire," I said. "You already seem to be sure you can. What makes you so certain you can afford to?"

Jim and Sue exchanged a look. Then Jim turned back to me. "You don't think we're rich enough," he said, "do you?" The way Jim put it, it wasn't exactly a question.

"Well, that's not the way I would have phrased it," I replied, "but yes, it takes a fair amount of money to fund an early retirement, and most people your age aren't even close to having saved enough. Knowing what I do about your background, I'm truthfully curious about how you could possibly have enough money." I looked him in the eye. He gazed back at me serenely.

"Jim, you're only fifty-two." I said. "Considering that only about one in ten people can barely afford to retire at age sixty-five with a lifestyle equal to what they had when they worked, you have to admit that retiring at your age with your income would be a pretty big feat."

Jim nodded. "Fair enough," he said and handed me a sheaf of documents. They included his and Sue's tax returns as well as financial statements that listed exactly what they owned and owed.

I looked first at their tax returns. The previous year, Jim and Sue had earned a total of $53,946. Not bad. Not rich, to be sure, but a decent income.

Okay, next. How much did they owe?

I scanned their financial statements. I couldn't find any outstanding debts listed. "Hmm," I said, raising an eyebrow. "You have no debt?"

"THE MCINTYRES DON'T DO DEBT."

They exchanged another smile, and Sue squeezed Jim's hand. "The McIntyres don't do debt," she said with a chuckle.

"What about your kids?" I asked.

"What about them?" Jim answered. "They're both out of college, on their own, and God bless 'em."

"Well, all right then," I said, "let's see what you own." I turned back to the financial statement. There were two homes listed: the house where they lived (valued at $450,000) and a rental property (a second house valued at $325,000).

"Wow," I said. "Two houses and no mortgage on either?"

"Nope," Jim replied. "No mortgage."

Next came the retirement accounts. Jim's 401(k) balance currently amounted to $610,000. And there was more. Sue had two retirement accounts of her own that totaled $72,000. In addition, they owned $160,000 in municipal bonds and had $62,500 in cash in a bank savings account.

Talk about a substantial asset base. Add in some personal property (including a boat and three cars—all fully paid for) and they had a net worth approaching $2 million!

By any standard, the McIntyres were rich. It wasn't simply that they owned a lot of assets free and clear (though that in itself was pretty impressive); they also had a continuing stream of income in the form of interest and dividends from their investments and $26,000 a year in rent generated by their second house. On top of that, Jim had qualified for a small pension, and Sue liked being a beautician so much that she planned to keep working until she was sixty (even though she didn't need to). Suddenly, Jim's plan to retire at fifty-two didn't seem so crazy. In fact, it was completely realistic. More than realistic—it was exciting!

"WE INHERITED KNOWLEDGE."

Normally, I don't get wide-eyed about people's wealth. But there was something about the McIntyres that impressed me. They didn't look rich. And they didn't seem terribly special. To the contrary, they seemed perfectly ordinary—your average, nice, hardworking couple. How could they have possibly amassed such wealth at such a relatively young age?

To put it mildly, I was confused. But I was also hooked. I was in my mid-twenties at the time, and even though I was making good money, I was still basically living paycheck to paycheck. Some months I did manage to save a little, but more often than not I'd get busy or spend too much the next month and not save a dime. Many months it seemed that instead of getting ahead, I was falling behind, working harder and harder to make ends meet.

It was embarrassing, really, and frustrating. Here I was, a financial advisor teaching others how to invest, and I was often struggling myself. Even worse, here were the McIntyres, who probably in their best year barely made half of what I was making, and yet they were millionaires, while I was falling further and further into debt.

Clearly, they knew something about taking action with their money that I needed to learn. And I was determined to find out what it was. How could such regular people have amassed such wealth? Eager to know their secret but not knowing where to begin, I finally asked them, "Did you inherit any of this?"

Jim broke out in a deep belly laugh. "Inherit?" he repeated, shaking his head. "The only thing we inherited was knowledge. Our parents taught us a few commonsense rules about handling money. We just did what they said, and sure enough it worked. The same is true for a lot of people we know. In fact, in our neighborhood, about half our friends are going to retire this year, and many of them are even better off then we are."

At this point, I was hooked. The McIntyres had come to interview me about how I could help them, but now I wanted to interview them.

LOOKING RICH VS. BEING RICH

"You know," I said, "every week I meet people who take my classes like you did but who are exactly the opposite of you. I mean, they look rich, but when you get into the details of what they really have, it often turns out that they are not only *not* rich but broke. Just this morning, I met with a man who drove up in a brand-new Porsche, wearing a gold Rolex watch. He looked loaded, but when I went through his statements I found he was actually leveraged to the hilt. A guy in his mid-fifties, living in a million-dollar home with an $800,000 mortgage. Less than $100,000 in savings, more than $75,000 in credit card debt, and he was leasing the Porsche! Plus he was paying alimony to two ex-wives."

At this point, the three of us couldn't help ourselves. We all began to laugh. "I know it's not funny," I said, "but here was this guy, looking rich and successful, and actually he's a financial and emotional wreck. He handled his finances just like he drove his Porsche: redlining all the way. Then you guys come in. You drive up in a Ford Taurus. Jim here is wearing a ten-year-old Timex—"

"Nope," Jim interrupted with a smile. "It's an eighteen-year-old Timex."

"Exactly!" I said. "An eighteen-year-old Timex. And you're *rich.* You guys are happy as clams, still married, two great kids you put through college, and you're retiring in your mid-fifties. So please tell me—what was your secret? You must have one, right?"

Sue looked me straight in the eye. "You really want to know?" she asked.

I nodded wordlessly. Sue looked at Jim. "You think we can spare an extra fifteen minutes to explain it to him?"

"Sure," Jim said. "What's fifteen minutes?" He turned to me. "You know, David, you already know this stuff. You teach it every day. We just lived it."

JIM AND SUE SHARE THEIR STORY

Sue took a deep breath, then launched into their story. "Well, first, we got married young. Jimmy was twenty-one when we started dating, and I was nineteen. We were married three years later. After our honeymoon, both of our parents sat us down and told us together that we needed to get serious with our lives. They said we had a choice. We could work all our lives for money and live month to month, paycheck to paycheck, like most people. Or we could learn to make our money work for us and really enjoy our lives. The trick, they said, was simple. Every time you earn a dollar, you should make sure to pay yourself first."

"WE DECIDED TO PAY OURSELVES FIRST."

Jim nodded in agreement. "You know," he said, "most people think that when they get their paycheck, the first thing they should do is pay all their bills—and then if there is anything left over, they can save a few dollars. In other words, pay everyone else first and yourself last. Our parents taught us that to really get ahead of the game, you have to turn this around. Put aside a few dollars for yourself, THEN pay all your other bills."

He sat back in his chair and shrugged, as if to say, "No big deal."

Sue smiled and shook her head. "Jim makes it sound easy," she said, "but the truth is we had to learn how to save our money. In the beginning, we tried to put ourselves on a budget, but somehow the numbers never added up and we started fighting a lot. One day I called my mom, upset because of a money fight we'd had, and she told me that budgeting didn't work. She said she and my dad had tried it and all it had led to was endless arguments. So they decided to toss the budget and instead take 10 percent of their pay out of their paychecks and put it in a savings account before they ever saw it or had a chance to spend it on anything. 'You'd be surprised how quickly you get used to doing without that 10 percent,' she told me. 'And meanwhile it's piling up in the bank.' The secret, she explained, is that you can't spend what you don't see.

"So that's what we did. We originally started by putting aside just 4 percent of our income and slowly increased the amount. Today, we save 15 percent. But on average we always saved about 10 percent, just like Mom said."

"And what did you do with your savings?" I asked.

"Well," Sue said, "the first thing we started saving for was our retirement."

"You know, back then we didn't have 401(k) plans," Jim broke in. "But a lot of companies, including mine, had pension plans that allowed you to contribute extra money if you wanted to. Most of our friends didn't bother. But we did."

Sue took up the story again. "After that, our next priority was to put aside enough so we could buy a home. Both our parents told us that their homes had been the best investments they had ever made—that nothing gives you freedom and security like owning a home. But the key, they said, was owning it free and clear. In other words, you pay off that mortgage as quickly as you can.

"They said that while our friends were busy splurging on decorating their apartments and eating lunch out every day, we should be watching our spending and saving as much as we could. They made a big point about how so many people waste big money on small things."

She looked at Jim. "You remember that, honey?" she asked.

"I sure do," Jim replied. He turned to me. "You know, the trick to getting ahead financially isn't being cheap and boring. It's watching the small stuff—little spending habits you have that you'd probably be better off without. In our case, we realized that one of the main 'small stuff' things we were spending too much money on were cigarettes. We both smoked about a pack a day and our parents hated it. Back then, the health risks were just beginning to be publicized, and they pointed out that if we stopped wasting money on cigarettes we could probably save enough in two years to make a down payment on a home. And we'd be saving our health in the process."

"WE WATCHED OUR LATTE FACTOR."

Jim leaned forward in his chair. "You know that concept in your seminars that you call The Latte Factor, where you teach people to stop wasting money on expensive coffee each morning and instead invest it?"

I nodded.

"Well, my dad didn't call it that, but it was the same thing. He could have called it the Cigarette Factor or the 'Don't be dumb with your money' factor. The idea was identical. If we saved a few dollars a day, we could eventually buy our own home. He said if we rented we would always be poor, making someone else rich. If we bought a home, we'd eventually make ourselves rich."

"That's it?" I asked. "You saved some money by cutting out cigarettes and bought a home?" I looked at Jim and Sue. They smiled back at me and nodded. "But how did you end up with two homes, both mortgage-free?"

"Well, we don't really have two homes," Sue said. "We've

got one home and a rental property. That was another part of the secret."

Jim took up the story. "Our parents taught us a trick that makes it easy to pay down your mortgage early. It's something you will love but will require more work from your bank. These days it's easier than ever. What you do is take your mortgage payment and instead of paying it in full once a month, you pay half every two weeks. You do that consistently, and by the end of the year you've made a whole extra payment without ever feeling the pinch. So instead of taking thirty years to pay down your mortgage, you'll have the thing paid off in twenty-three years. We figured that by following this plan we could buy a home in our mid-twenties and own it free and clear by the time we were in our late forties. What actually happened was even better. We ended up making even more extra mortgage payments on a consistent basis. So by the time we were in our late thirties, the house was pretty well paid off."

"So then what?" I asked.

"Then we didn't have any more mortgage payments to make, and without them, we had all this extra money each month." Jim grinned at me. "We figured either we could waste it or we could buy a nicer house and rent out our first one. So that's what we did, using the same trick with the payment schedule to pay off the mortgage faster. Bingo—next thing you know, we own two homes free and clear: one to live in, the other to rent out for a nice, steady stream of extra income."

"Good plan," I said.

Jim nodded vigorously. "Another thing Sue's mom and dad taught us was never to buy on credit," he said. "They had a strict policy, which they passed along to us, and which we've passed along to our kids: No matter how big they are, you pay for your purchases with cash or you don't buy. The only exception is buying a house, and, like Sue said, you pay off the mortgage as quickly as you can. It's not always easy, but that's the rule."

"That's right," Sue chimed in. "It took Jim five years of saving to be able to buy that boat of his."

"And even then, I chose to buy a used one," he added. "But that's okay. I was perfectly happy to let someone else make the mistake of buying it new at full price—and then letting me have it for a fraction of what he paid. We did the same thing with all our cars. We always bought used, and never regretted it. You have the car checked out by a reliable mechanic, take good care of it, and it'll run just fine."

"The point is," Sue said, "if we didn't have enough cash to buy something, we didn't buy it. The entire time we've been married, we've never carried credit card debt. When we used the cards, we paid them off the same month. That was another tip our parents gave us that they said we'd love and the banks would not."

THE MOST IMPORTANT SECRET

I sat back in my chair, amazed at how simple the McIntyres made it all seem. There had to be a catch. I thought about it for a moment, and then I realized what it was. "Everything you're talking about," I said, "it all makes sense. Cutting out wasteful spending, accelerating your mortgage payments, paying yourself first, buying only with cash, avoiding credit card debt—you're absolutely right. These are all things I teach in my seminars. But to put it all together the way you have must have taken phenomenal will power. Seriously, my hat is off to you. I wish everyone had the kind of self-discipline you guys clearly possess. Unfortunately, most of us don't. I guess that's why most people never become rich the way you have."

Once again, Jim and Sue exchanged glances. They both smiled, and Jim gestured for Sue to explain.

YOU DON'T NEED WILL POWER OR DISCIPLINE

"But that's just the point," she began. "We *don't* have phenomenal will power. If following our parents' tips had been a matter of self-discipline, I don't think we would have done nearly as well as we have."

"I don't think we would have done well at all," interrupted Jim. "I mean, Sue has some self-control, but me—forget about it."

Now I was really confused. "I don't get it," I said. "If you don't have any special self-discipline, how did you do it? After all, we live in a society in which advertising and entertainment—even the government—are constantly bombarding us with temptations to do exactly the opposite of everything your parents taught you to do. So how did you resist? How did you get yourselves to stick to all those rules in the face of all that temptation?"

I was asking out of more than just professional curiosity. As I said, I was in my mid-twenties at the time, and I was personally finding it incredibly hard to be disciplined enough to save the kind of money I knew I should be saving. My intense desire to know must have shown in my face, because both Jim and Sue suddenly burst out laughing. After a moment, I joined in too.

"You know, David," Jim said finally, "we have a daughter who's just a little bit younger than you. So believe it or not, we do understand how hard it can be to be disciplined about saving money when you're in your twenties. But that's the beauty of our approach. It doesn't require discipline."

I gave him a doubtful look.

"I'm not surprised you're skeptical," Jim said. "It's so simple and obvious that even someone who knows as much about money as you do has a hard time seeing it. Here's the thing. Let's say you know you should do something, but you're afraid you may be tempted to do something else. How can you make sure you do the right thing?"

Jim looked at me. I shrugged.

"Like I said," he continued, "it's simple and obvious. You take the decision out of your hands. You arrange to have the thing you should do happen automatically."

"Remember what I was telling you before, about how we started paying ourselves first?" Sue interjected. "What we did was arrange to have a portion of our pay automatically taken out of our paychecks and put in a savings account. The key thing was that it was all automatic. Once we'd set it up, we didn't have to do a thing. It was out of our hands—literally."

"Of course," I said. "It's just like the systematic savings and investment programs I talk about in my class. Except you apply it to every aspect of your finances."

"Exactly!" Jim exclaimed. "If you don't have to think about it, there's no chance you'll forget to do it—or, worse, change your mind and deliberately *not* do it. Once the decision is out of your hands, there's no way you can be tempted into doing the wrong thing."

"WE DECIDED TO BECOME AUTOMATIC MILLIONAIRES."

It was Sue's turn again. "Our parents called it protecting yourself from yourself," she said. "We didn't have to worry about having any special will power, because we really didn't have to do anything except decide at the beginning that we wanted to be rich. With the help of this great thing called 'payroll deduction,' we made everything automatic. We created a literally foolproof automatic system to achieve wealth.

"We had Jim's company take money out of his paycheck and invest it in his retirement account. We handled our accelerated mortgage payments in a similar fashion. The minute the banks started offering automatic transfer programs, we got ours to take our monthly mortgage payment—plus a little extra—right out of our checking account without our having to do or say anything. We also used a systematic deduction scheme to automatically invest a portion of both our incomes in mutual funds. Eventually, we even automated our tithing. We always used to give a little each year to charity, but as time went on we realized how simple it would be to make the process automatic."

"Understand," Jim said, "we're not talking about huge amounts of money. At the beginning, I was having less than fifty dollars a month deducted from my paycheck. But over time it really adds up."

I glanced down at the McIntyres' financial statements, with their seven-figure net worth. "You're not kidding," I said. "It really is remarkable."

Sue McIntyre shook her head. "That's where you're wrong," she said quietly. "It's not remarkable. If we can do it, anyone can do it. By deciding to be rich at a young age, and then, by creating an automatic system for wealth, we made it impossible to fail. It's like the Nike slogan, with a twist. They say, 'Just do it.' We say, 'Just do it . . . once.' When it comes to money, all you have to do is automate your system and you're done."

Jim nodded in agreement. "You know, back when we started, the technology of doing things automatically was new and most of our friends didn't trust it. But today, it's a no-brainer. I mean, with all the programs they have now, you can automate everything you do financially in literally minutes. Our daughter Lucy got everything set up for herself in less than half an hour. Now she's all on her way to becoming an automatic millionaire just like us."

"And don't think," Sue said, laughing, "that you have to be a couple of old fogies like we are to make it work. You'll excuse a mother for bragging, but our Lucy happens to be a very stylish young lady. No Timex on *her* wrist."

"Yeah." Jim grinned. "She's got one of those Swatches. Very fashionable and all, but not ridiculously expensive."

"And that's the point," Sue said. "You can save and still have fun and look great. You don't have to become a stick-in-the-mud in order to get rich. We certainly weren't. We've had a blast together the last thirty years, as much fun as our friends, if not more, because our lives have been free from the stresses of worrying every day about money."

The McIntyres left my office the way they came in, hand in hand, looking forward to their future together with all the excitement of a newlywed couple. I sat at my desk for a long time, thinking about what they had told me—especially Jim and Sue's parting words.

The key, they said, was to "set yourself up for success." Why make getting rich hard, they said, when you can make getting rich easy? They were right, I realized. As long as you know what to do and can arrange to do it "automatically," anyone can become an Automatic Millionaire.

That session with the McIntyres was a turning point in my life. It made me realize the one crucial step to creating a lasting, positive change in the way you handle your money.

MAKE IT AUTOMATIC!

As a result of what I learned that day with the McIntyres, I automated everything I was doing financially. And you know what? It worked. Today, I too am an Automatic Millionaire.

NOW IT'S YOUR TURN

The story of the McIntyres and how they got rich without discipline by amassing wealth slowly and steadily can become your story. To find out how, turn the page and continue reading. You are a few hours away from a new way of thinking and a new way of handling your hard-earned money.

You are on your way to becoming an Automatic Millionaire.

CHAPTER TWO

THE LATTE FACTOR:

Becoming an Automatic Millionaire on Just a Few Dollars a Day

"The problem is not how much we earn . . . it's how much we spend!"

So where do we begin?

Probably not where you think.

Most people believe that the secret to getting rich is all about finding new ways of increasing their income as quickly as possible. "If only I could make more money," they declare, "I'd be rich." How many times have you heard somebody say that? How many times have you said it yourself? Well, it simply isn't true. Ask anyone who got a raise last year if their savings increased. In almost every case, the answer will be no.

Why? Because more often than not, **the more we make, the more we spend.**

There are a lot of lessons we can all learn from the McIntyres, but if you take only one thing away from their story, it should be this: *How much you earn has almost no bearing on whether or not you can and will build wealth.* Remember what Jim McIntyre told me: He never talked about how much money he made at his job or with his investments. The trick to getting ahead financially, he said, is watching the small stuff—little spending habits you have that you'd probably be better off without.

Most people have a hard time believing this. Why? Because they are taught the opposite. We live in a society where it's become almost patriotic to spend every penny of our paychecks. In fact, we often spend our pay increases even before we get them. Merchandisers know this; they run ads every November and December specifically designed to get people to spend their year-end bonuses. Even the government promotes this idea. The way to pump up the economy, say the politicians, is to cut taxes—the idea being that if you put a little extra money in people's pockets, they'll naturally go out and spend it.

Unfortunately, there's a problem with this. If you are living paycheck to paycheck, spending everything you make, what you're really doing is running an unwinnable race.

Here's what the race looks like:

GO TO WORK . . . MAKE MONEY . . . SPEND MONEY . . .
GO TO WORK . . . MAKE MONEY . . . SPEND MONEY . . .
GO TO WORK . . .

Notice how it always comes back to GO TO WORK. This is the endless treadmill that most people are on. Some people call it the "rat race." It's a race in which hardworking people bust their butts, working forty to fifty hours a week or more—and wind up with almost nothing to show for it because at the end of the month their paycheck is already spent.

It's an unfair, vicious cycle, and you don't want to fall into it. If you are already there, you want to get out . . . fast. When you spend everything you make (or, worse, spend *more* than you make), you subject yourself to a life of stress, fear, uncertainty, debt, and even worse—bankruptcy and the threat of future poverty.

ARE YOU EARNING MORE . . . AND SAVING LESS?

Over the years, I've watched people I love increase their earnings but often not their freedom. I've got one friend who's worked extremely hard and seen his income go from $50,000 a year to more than $500,000. But while his lifestyle has increased along with his income, his savings haven't. He has nicer clothes and nicer cars, eats at fancier restaurants, shops at fancier stores, goes on fancier trips, but he's not really any wealthier. In fact, he's actually more stressed today than he was ten years ago because now he's got this expensive lifestyle to support—with the country club membership, the nanny, the private schools for the kids, and the big mortgage—and he can't imagine living without it. He's succeeding at a level that most Americans can only dream about, but in reality he's caught up in the same rat race as a person who earns a fraction of his salary.

What about you? Chances are that you're earning more than you were ten years ago. But are you saving more? Are you getting ahead or running harder just to stay even. Is your income helping you become more free or less free?

WHY MOST AMERICANS HAVE SO LITTLE SAVED

Aside from the equity they may have in their homes, most Americans really don't have any savings to speak of. On average, most of us have less than three months' worth of expenses in the bank.

Why so little? The answer is simple. As Jim and Sue McIntyre's parents taught them, most of us waste a lot of what we earn on "small things." I put quotation marks around "small things" because the phrase is misleading. The so-called small things on which we waste money every day can add up in a hurry to life-changing amounts that ultimately can cost us our freedom.

I OWE, I OWE . . . IT'S OFF TO WORK I GO

It doesn't have to be this way. Most of us don't really think about how we spend our money—and if we do, we often focus solely on the big-ticket items while ignoring the small daily expenses that drain away our cash. We don't think about how many hours we had to work to earn the money that we so casually spend on this or that "small thing." Even worse, we don't realize how much wealth we might have if, instead of wasting our income, we invested just a little of it.

By coming to understand what I call The Latte Factor, you are now going to change all of that. Like the McIntyres, you're going to become more aware of how much you are wasting on "small things"—and how to redirect that wasted money to help you build a fortune. It doesn't matter if you earn what you think of as a small paycheck. Regardless of how big or small your income is, by making use of The Latte Factor you can start to build real wealth and ultimately more freedom.

In short, with the help of The Latte Factor you can finally start doing what the rich do—**you can get your money to work for you, instead of your working for it.**

"A latte spurned is a fortune earned."
—*People* magazine

Over the past few years, The Latte Factor has become an internationally recognized metaphor for how we dribble away what should be our fortunes on small things without ever really giving it much thought. The idea has been featured in magazines and newspapers and on television and radio shows around the world. You may have seen it discussed in a feature article in *People,* or read about it *USA Today, Business Week,* or *Family Circle.* I've talked about it with Oprah Winfrey on *The*

Oprah Winfrey Show, Barbara Walters on *The View* and demonstrated it on NBC's *Today* show and on CNBC and CNN.

Before we get into the details of The Latte Factor and the power it can have in your life, it's important that you understand one thing. In order to become an Automatic Millionaire, you've got to accept the idea that regardless of the size of your paycheck, you probably already make enough money to become rich. I can't stress enough the importance of believing this—not just with your mind but with your heart as well. It's an "Aha!" moment that can truly change your life financially.

WHAT IS THE LATTE FACTOR?

The Latte Factor is based on something that actually happened to me about ten years ago. One day, with about fifteen minutes left in the last session of a four-week investment course I was teaching, a young woman named Kim raised her hand and said something that stopped me in my tracks.

"David," she announced, "your ideas are good in theory, but they don't have anything to do with reality."

Needless to say, I did not enjoy hearing this. "What do you mean?" I asked her. "How can you say that?"

"Very easily," Kim replied. "You see, David, you make this idea of saving money seem easy, but in reality it's impossible. You talk about saving five to ten dollars a day like it's no big deal. Well, for me, it *is* a big deal. In fact, it's impossible. I'm living paycheck to paycheck. I mean, I'm barely making ends meet each month. So how can I possibly save five to ten dollars a day? It's just not realistic."

THE IMPOSSIBLE MADE POSSIBLE

With just about everyone else in the class nodding in agreement, I threw out my lesson plan and decided to devote the rest of the time we had left to answering Kim's question.

"Kim," I began, "because obviously there are others in this room who feel the same way you do, let's really look at what you're saying. Will you work with me here?"

"Sure," Kim said.

"Great," I replied. I turned to the blackboard and picked up a piece of chalk. "Let's go through your expenses for a typical day. Walk me through everything you do in the course of the day."

"Well," she said, "I go to work and then I answer messages from the day before—"

"Hold on," I interrupted. "What about before you get to the office? Do you start your day with coffee?"

The woman sitting next to Kim looked at her and laughed. "Kim without coffee in the morning," she said, shaking her head, "not a safe thing."

Kim poked her friend, then turned back to me. "Yes," she said, "I start my day with coffee."

"Okay," I replied. "Is it coffee you make at home, or do you get it at the office for free?"

It quickly came out that Kim generally stopped at Starbucks every morning to get her coffee. Actually, she and her friend went together. It was their special "girls' gift" to themselves.

"Great," I said. "Now, do you get a regular coffee?"

"Well, no," Kim replied. "I always get a double nonfat latte."

I nodded thoughtfully. "I'm curious. Just what does this double nonfat latte cost you every morning?"

"Three fifty," came the answer.

"And is that it, Kim? Do you get anything to eat with your latte? Maybe a bagel?"

"Actually, I get a muffin."

"Great. And that costs?"

"A buck fifty," Kim's friend volunteered. "I know because I get one too!"

The class cracked up. As the laughter died down, a guy in the front of the room turned and asked, "How in the world does a muffin cost a dollar fifty?"

"Well, they're fat-free," Kim said.

Everyone started laughing again. Even Kim.

Meanwhile I turned to the blackboard and wrote down the following:

Double Nonfat Latte	$3.50
Nonfat Muffin	$1.50
Total	$5.00

"Interesting," I said, looking back at Kim. "Not even at work yet and you've already spent five dollars. Okay, keep going."

Kim seemed a little annoyed. "Look," she said, "everyone

does it. It's not a big deal. I mean, give me a break. As hard as I work, I should be able to treat myself to a cup of coffee."

I threw up my hands in mock surrender. "It's not a big deal, Kim. Just keep going, okay? What else do you do during the day?"

Kim looked at me for a moment, then got back into the swing of things. "Well, I take a break at ten A.M., usually with a few friends, and we go get a juice."

"Oh, really? And what's the juice cost?"

"Well, it costs three ninety-five."

Kim's friend spoke up again. "Yeah," she said, "but, Kim, you usually add that brain stuff to it. You know, that Kinko babalooey stuff?"

"It's not Kinko babalooey," Kim snapped at her. "It's Ginkgo biloba, and it's proven to increase the oxygen supply to your brain."

"Well," I said, "now that we know you have oxygen in the brain, out of curiosity, what does it cost to add Ginkgo biloba to your drink?"

"The 'juice boost' is fifty cents more," Kim said, still glaring at her friend.

"Anything to eat with it?" I asked.

"Yes. By ten, I'm usually starving. After all, the only thing I've had to eat is that nonfat muffin."

"So what do you get?"

"I get a PowerBar and it costs me one seventy-five." Kim folded her arms and looked at me, as if daring me to make a comment. "Okay?"

I nodded and turned back to the blackboard.

Double Nonfat Latte	$3.50
Nonfat Muffin	$1.50
Juice	$3.95
Juice Boost	.50
PowerBar	$1.75
Total	$11.20

"So, Kim," I said, "we're not even at lunch yet and you've spent more than ten dollars. And truth be told, you haven't really had anything to eat yet!"

Now the class was laughing pretty hard. Including Kim and her friend.

I waited for the laughter to subside, then said, "Seriously, Kim, we don't need to go through the rest of your day in front of the class. You can do that later. The point here is not to make fun of how you spend money. The only reason everyone is laughing is that we all know we're just as bad with our money as you are. We may not like to admit it, but we all spend small amounts of money every day and never think of what it adds up to. But let me show you something that I think will amaze you."

I pulled out my calculator. "Let's say, for the sake of argument, that today, this very day, you started to save money. I'm not saying you cut out all your spending—just that you reduced it a little. Let's say you realized you could save five dollars a day? Can we try that? Just five dollars a day, okay?"

Kim nodded.

"Now you are . . . how old?"

"Twenty-three," Kim said.

"Okay, let's say you put five dollars a day into a retirement plan." I punched some figures into the calculator. "That equals $150 a month, or almost $2,000 a year. Figuring, say, a 10 percent annual return, which is what the stock market has averaged over the last fifty years, how much do you think you could save by the time you're sixty-five?"

Kim shrugged. "I don't know," she said. "Maybe a hundred thousand?"

I shook my head.

Kim started to guess. "Two hundred thousand?"

"Try again," I said.

"Five hundred thousand?"

"How about nearly $1.2 million."

Kim stared at me, her eyes wide.

"And that's actually a low-ball estimate," I said. "As I recall, you work for a company that matches employee contributions to a 401(k) plan. That's right, isn't it?"

Kim nodded.

"Well, if your company matched just 50 percent of what you put in, you'd actually be saving close to $3,000 a year. And by the time you're sixty-five that would add up to"—I punched some more figures into my calculator—"roughly $1,742,467!"

At this point, I could see the imaginary light bulb go off over Kim's head. "David," she said finally, "are you trying to tell me that **MY LATTES ARE COSTING ME NEARLY TWO MILLION DOLLARS!**"

In unison, virtually everyone in the room (including Kim's friend) looked at her and cried out, "YES!"

And so The Latte Factor was born.

WHAT IF I DON'T DRINK COFFEE?

No sooner had the hubbub died down than a man in the back row raised his hand and said, "But, David, I don't drink coffee. I would never waste the kind of money she wastes on lattes. That's ridiculous."

I nodded. His was an understandable reaction, but it missed the point. "Folks," I said to him and the class, "what we're talking about here isn't just lattes. And I'm not picking on Starbucks. In fact, I go there sometimes myself. What we're talking about is how we don't realize how much we spend on little things and how, if we thought about it and changed our habits just a little, we could change our destiny."

Someone else had another question. "But what if your investments don't earn 10 percent a year like you figured for Kim?"

"No problem," I said. "Say you got an annual return of only 6 percent. You'd still wind up with hundreds of thousands of dollars in savings." I did some more quick figuring on my calculator. "In Kim's case, the total would be $559,523. The bottom line here is that saving small amounts of money can make you rich. And the sooner you start, the better."

By then, it was way past when the class should have ended. And still people hung around to talk. It seemed that of everything I had taught them during the previous four weeks, the thing that really hit home was how much money Kim's morning latte was really costing her. As my students walked off to their cars, chatting about what their individual Latte Factors might be, it occurred to me that The Latte Factor was something I should probably share again.

When I prepared for my new class the next week, I created a visual to illustrate the power of The Latte Factor. I've been using it ever since. Here's what it looks like.

A LATTE A DAY KEEPS RETIREMENT AWAY		
A Latte a Day	=	$3.50
A Latte a Day for a Month	=	$105.00
A Latte a Day for a Year	=	$1,260.00
A Latte a Day for a Decade	=	$12,600.00

What else do people waste money on?

What about cigarettes? These little things aren't just a health risk; they are also a financial risk. In New York City, where I live, cigarettes are taxed so heavily that a pack now costs more than seven dollars. Still, hundreds of thousands of people—particularly young adults—buy them every day.

A PACK OF CIGARETTES A DAY . . . IS EVEN WORSE		
A Pack a Day	=	$7
A Pack a Day for a Month	=	$210
A Pack a Day for a Year	=	$2,520
A Pack a Day for a Decade	=	$25,200

I could go on and on, but these two examples should suffice. And, again, I'm not picking on coffee or cigarettes. I'm just showing you the numbers. It's all in the math. And it's basic math (thank goodness, because I'm no math whiz, and you don't need to be one either).

The point is that whether you waste money on fancy coffee, bottled water (now that's a funny one), cigarettes, soft drinks, candy bars, fast food, or whatever it happens to be—we all have a Latte Factor. We all throw away too much of our hard-earned money on unnecessary "little" expenditures without realizing how much they can add up to. The sooner you figure out your Latte Factor—that is, identify those unnecessary expenditures—the sooner you can start eliminating them. And the sooner you do that, the more extra money you'll be able to put aside. And the more extra money you can put aside, the larger the fortune you'll wind up amassing.

Consider this:

USE THE POWER OF THE LATTE FACTOR

$5 (average cost of a latte and a muffin) × 7 days = $35/week = approx. $150/month. If you invested $150 a month and earned 10% annual return, you'd wind up with

1 year	=	$1,885
2 years	=	$3,967
5 years	=	$11,616
10 years	=	$30,727
15 years	=	$62,171
30 years	=	$339,073
40 years	=	$948,611

Interesting, isn't it? Now, what if you took this a step further and said, "You know, I bet I waste ten dollars a day on things I don't really need to buy." What would that look like?

If you invested $10 a day (or $300/month) and earned 10% annual return, you'd wind up with

1 year	=	$3,770
2 years	=	$7,934
5 years	=	$23,231
10 years	=	$61,453
15 years	=	$124,341
30 years	=	$678,146
40 years	=	$1,897,224

Let's try it one more time. What if you were in a committed relationship, married or living together, and the two of you looked at this and said, "You know what—let's go for it. Let's *each* save ten dollars a day." What could happen?

If you invested $20 a day (or $600/month) and earned 10% annual return, you'd wind up with

1 year	=	$7,539
2 years	=	$15,868
5 years	=	$46,462
10 years	=	$122,907
15 years	=	$248,682
30 years	=	$1,356,293
40 years	=	$3,794,448

Now, let that sink in. Really look at those numbers and think about it. Is it possible that you could find five to ten dollars that you could cut out of your daily spending?

I think you'll find the answer is yes. Keep in mind that all we're talking about here is saving less than one hour's worth of pay for yourself each day. If you are going to put in roughly

90,000 hours at work over the course of your lifetime (which is what the average person does), shouldn't you work one hour a day for yourself? At the very least, it's something to think about.

THERE ARE NO TRICKS HERE

Becoming rich requires nothing more than committing and sticking to a systematic savings and investment plan. If you're not particularly disciplined, don't worry. Over the next few chapters, you are going to learn how to make your plan "automatic," just like the McIntyres did. For now, I just want you to focus on the fact that you don't need to have a lot of money or earn a lot of money. You just need to make the decision that you deserve to be rich. You just need to say to yourself, "You know what? I should have financial freedom. Other people do. Why not me? Why not now?"

YEAH, BUT . . . YEAH, BUT . . . YEAH, BUT . . .

This is where the "yeah, buts" come in. What's a "yeah, but"? It's what people do all the time to rationalize their current place in life. And what's so funny (and sad) about "yeah, but-ers" is that they often try really hard to find ways to improve their situation—only to "yeah, but" their way right past the answers.

How do you know if you're a "yeah, but-er"? You probably are one if you're talking to yourself right now and saying things like:

Yeah, but . . . I'll never be able to earn a 10 percent return on my money.

Wrong. Later on, I'll share with you how to do this over time. Just keep reading.

Yeah, but . . . with inflation and all, $1 million won't be worth much in thirty years.

Wrong. It will be worth more than you think. And it will certainly be worth a lot more than nothing—which is what you'll have if you don't start putting money aside now.

Yeah, but . . . there really isn't a way to save small amounts of money and invest it. You need a lot more dough than that to be able to invest.

Wrong. These days you can set up automatic investment plans with as little as a dollar a day. Just keep reading.

Yeah, but . . . I really know for a fact that I don't waste a penny and there's no way for me to save the kind of money you're talking about.

Oh, come on. Hit yourself in the head (gently) and just keep reading. What you're saying is just not true.

I WISH I'D SEEN THIS EARLIER

Here's one last chart for you to look at, and then we'll begin exploring how you can make The Latte Factor work for you. This chart is one of the most powerful savings motivators I've

THE TIME VALUE OF MONEY—Invest Now Rather Than Later

	Billy Investing at Age 15 (10% Annual Return)			Susan Investing at Age 19 (10% Annual Return)			Kim Investing at Age 27 (10% Annual Return)	
Age	Invest $3K/yr	Value	Age	Invest $3K/yr	Value	Age	Invest $3K/yr	Value
15	$3K	$3,300.00	15			15		
16	$3K	$6,930.00	16			16		
17	$3K	$10,923.00	17			17		
18	$3K	$15,315.30	18			18		
19	$3K	$20,146.83	19	$3K	$3,300.00	19		
20		$22,161.51	20	$3K	$6,930.00	20		
21		$24,377.66	21	$3K	$10,923.00	21		
22		$26,815.43	22	$3K	$15,315.30	22		
23		$29,496.97	23	$3K	$20,146.83	23		
24		$32,446.67	24	$3K	$25,461.51	24		
25		$35,691.34	25	$3K	$31,307.66	25		
26		$39,260.47	26	$3K	$37,738.43	26		
27		$43,186.52	27		$41,512.27	27	$3K	$3,300.00
28		$47,505.17	28		$45,663.50	28	$3K	$6,930.00
29		$52,255.69	29		$50,229.85	29	$3K	$10,923.00
30		$57,481.26	30		$55,252.84	30	$3K	$15,315.30
31		$63,229.38	31		$60,778.12	31	$3K	$20,146.83
32		$69,552.32	32		$66,855.93	32	$3K	$25,461.51
33		$76,507.55	33		$73,541.53	33	$3K	$31,307.66
34		$84,158.31	34		$80,895.68	34	$3K	$37,738.43
35		$92,574.14	35		$88,985.25	35	$3K	$44,812.27
36		$101,831.55	36		$97,883.77	36	$3K	$52,593.50
37		$112,014.71	37		$107,672.15	37	$3K	$61,152.85
38		$123,216.18	38		$118,439.36	38	$3K	$70,568.14
39		$135,537.80	39		$130,283.30	39	$3K	$80,924.95
40		$149,091.58	40		$143,311.63	40	$3K	$92,317.45
41		$164,000.74	41		$157,642.79	41	$3K	$104,849.19
42		$180,400.81	42		$173,407.07	42	$3K	$118,634.11
43		$198,440.89	43		$190,747.78	43	$3K	$133,797.52
44		$218,284.98	44		$209,822.55	44	$3K	$150,477.27
45		$240,113.48	45		$230,804.81	45	$3K	$168,825.00
46		$264,124.82	46		$253,885.29	46	$3K	$189,007.50
47		$290,537.31	47		$279,273.82	47	$3K	$211,208.25
48		$319,591.04	48		$307,201.20	48	$3K	$235,629.07
49		$351,550.14	49		$337,921.32	49	$3K	$262,491.98
50		$386,705.16	50		$371,713.45	50	$3K	$292,041.18
51		$425,375.67	51		$408,884.80	51	$3K	$324,545.30
52		$467,913.24	52		$449,773.28	52	$3K	$360,299.83
53		$514,704.56	53		$494,750.61	53	$3K	$399,629.81
54		$566,175.02	54		$544,225.67	54	$3K	$442,892.79
55		$622,792.52	55		$598,648.24	55	$3K	$490,482.07
56		$685,071.77	56		$658,513.06	56	$3K	$542,830.27
57		$753,578.95	57		$724,364.36	57	$3K	$600,413.30
58		$828,936.84	58		$796,800.80	58	$3K	$663,754.63
59		$911,830.53	59		$876,480.88	59	$3K	$733,430.10
60		$1,003,013.58	60		$964,128.97	60	$3K	$810,073.11
61		$1,103,314.94	61		$1,060,541.87	61	$3K	$894,380.42
62		$1,213,646.43	62		$1,166,596.05	62	$3K	$987,118.46
63		$1,335,011.08	63		$1,283,255.66	63	$3K	$1,089,130.30
64		$1,468,512.18	64		$1,411,581.22	64	$3K	$1,201,343.33
65		**$1,615,363.40**	**65**		**$1,552,739.35**	**65**	**$3K**	**$1,324,777.67**

Total invested = $15,000
Billy's earnings beyond investment = $1,600,363.40

Total invested = $24,000
Susan's earnings beyond investment = $1,528,739.35

Total invested = $117,000
Kim's earnings beyond investment = $1,207,777.67

Returns on all investment products will fluctuate. Investment return and principal value will fluctuate and your investment value may be more or less than the original invested amount.

Billy invested $102,000 less than Kim and has $290,585.73 more!
START INVESTING EARLY!

ever seen. Indeed, I wish someone had shown it to me when I was in high school. If you're older, please share it with a young person you love. You may change his or her life forever.

What the chart shows is the power of putting $3,000 a year into a retirement account and then letting compound interest work its magic. I'll explain about retirement accounts in the next chapter. For now, just look at the numbers—specifically, how relatively little money you have to put in compared to how much you wind up with at the end. When I display this chart in my Finish Rich seminars, people often gasp and say, "If I'd only known this sooner."

Well, now you know! The miracle of compound interest is the Automatic Millionaire's power tool for wealth.

FINDING YOUR LATTE FACTOR

You can think about your Latte Factor and guesstimate it, or you can catalog your actual spending and know it for sure. Either way works. Knowing it for sure is probably better.

To know for a fact what your Latte Factor is, use The Latte Factor Challenge form on the next page to track your expenses for one day. Take this book with you everywhere you go tomorrow and write down every penny you spend the entire day.

This may not seem like much of an activity right now, but, having shared the idea with my students, readers, and clients for years, I can tell you that when you actually put it into action, this simple exercise can be life-changing. It is truly stun-

THE LATTE FACTOR CHALLENGE

DAY _____ DATE _____

	Item: What I bought	Cost: What I spent	Wasted Money? (✓for yes)
1			
2			
3			
4			
5			
6			
7			
8			
9			
10			
11			
12			
13			
14			
15			

My Latte Factor Total: (Total Cost of Checked Items)

= [   ]

THE LATTE FACTOR MATH

My Latte Factor for one day = _____

My Latte Factor for one month = _____ (Latte Factor x 30)

My Latte Factor for one year = _____ (Latte Factor x 365)

My Latte Factor for a decade = _____ (Latte Factor x 3,650)

IF I INVESTED MY LATTE FACTOR FOR:

10 years it would be worth = _____

20 years it would be worth = _____

30 years it would be worth = _____

40 years it would be worth = _____

CALCULATING YOUR LATTE FACTOR

To calculate the numbers above go to www.finishrich.com. Click on "calculators" and then click on "Apply the Latte Factor."

FREE! MY GIFT TO YOU

To win a free Latte Factor mug, share your Latte Factor experience by e-mailing us at success@finishrich.com. Just tell us what happened to you when you took the challenge. How much money did you find? What did you learn? Every day a winner will be selected!

---

ning to see in black and white just how much you spend—and on what—over the course of a single day. There is something about seeing it written down in cold, clear figures that can motivate you to make changes in the way you spend that you wouldn't normally make.

As an added bonus, you just might find that taking this small challenge is fun. You might find that during the day people ask you what you're doing. Your answer ("I'm tracking my Latte Factor") could spark a conversation that in turn might lead to your helping someone else become an Automatic Millionaire. And wouldn't that be something! After all, it's more fun to be rich with your friends than to be rich by yourself.

ANSWERS TO SOME FREQUENTLY ASKED QUESTIONS

Before we go any further, let me answer a few of the most frequently asked questions about The Latte Factor Challenge that I've gotten over the years.

One of the most popular questions is (and I swear this is

true) *David, should I include things I pay for with cash when I track my spending?*

The answer is yes.

What about credit cards and checks? Yes!

What about toll bridge fees? YES, YES, YES.

You track everything you spend. And everything means everything.

"OH, COME ON—THAT'S TOO DUMB."

A few years back, I described a seven-day version of The Latte Factor Challenge on a national radio show—and the host told me it was the dumbest idea he had ever heard. His exact words were, "Oh, come on—that's too dumb."

Considering this was a well-known radio show with a huge audience, I was a little upset by the host's put-down. "Come on, yourself," I said to him. "What's so stupid about it?"

He actually sneered at me. "Oh, David," he said, "it's cute and all, but get real. Track your expenses for seven days? Think about your Latte Factor? Give me a break. My audience needs real, concrete ideas. Not stupid gimmicks."

Now I was getting a little hot under the collar. I said, "You want something real? Well, how about this? How about you actually try this stupid idea of mine? You track your expenses for seven days, and then call me back in a week, live on the radio, and tell me if you still think it's so stupid. You do it seriously, and I bet you a hundred dollars it changes your life."

The host looked at me and grinned. "You're on," he said.

As it turned out, he didn't call me back a week later. So I

called him. He was a little surprised to hear from me, but he hadn't forgotten who I was or the bet we'd made. Sheepishly, he admitted that he had taken my Latte Factor Challenge. He said it had sickened him. You see, this national radio personality who knew it all and wanted concrete investment ideas for his audience told me that as a result of tracking his expenses for a week, he found out he was spending fifty dollars a day *just on eating out.* (For those of you who find this hard to believe, keep in mind that he lived in Manhattan and it's actually quite easy to spend that much in New York City.)

But what really stunned him was the math. After realizing that he had literally spent more than $350 that week on restaurant tabs, he started doing some basic arithmetic. "Do you realize what this means?" he said to me. "It means I'm spending $1,400 a month eating out. In a year, that's more than $16,800 eating out. Do you realize I have less than $20,000 in savings? I'm in my forties and I haven't put a dime in my 401(k) plan in nearly ten years because I don't feel I can afford it. I've been earning more than $100,000 a year for a decade and I have nothing to show for it."

He went on to tell me that because of what he had learned as a result of taking the challenge, he had just arranged to start making 401(k) contributions again. The Latte Factor had hit home for him.

My cute little idea had worked.

For some reason, however, he never had me back on his show.

MAYBE IT'S NOT SO DUMB?

At this point, I hope you are excited. Now let's see what you can do once you find your Latte Factor and take control of your spending. Your future is about to change permanently.

TAKING ACTION

First, let me say congratulations on reading this far. You've already read more pages of this little book on money than most people read in a lifetime. Well done.

From here on out, each chapter will end with a series of **Automatic Millionaire Action Steps.** These steps are meant to summarize what you just read and motivate you to take immediate, powerful action. Remember, inspiration unused is merely entertainment. To get new results, you need to take new actions. To become an Automatic Millionaire, you need to act on what you've learned. The only way to get the financial future you want is to begin creating it now!

AUTOMATIC MILLIONAIRE ACTION STEPS

Reviewing the actions we laid out in this chapter, here's what you should be doing right now to become an Automatic Millionaire. Check off each step as you accomplish it.

- ❑ Recognize that what matters is not how much you earn but how much you spend.

- ❑ Take The Latte Factor Challenge. For just one day, bring this book with you everywhere you go and use the form on page 50 to track everything you spend.

- ❑ Decide right now that you can live on a little less and start to save today.

- ❑ Study the charts on pages 44 and 45 or use The Latte Factor Calculator at www.finishrich.com to find out in seconds how much saving a few dollars a day can change your life.

CHAPTER THREE

LEARN TO
PAY YOURSELF
FIRST

Here's some great news. If The Latte Factor opened you to the possibility that you already make enough money to start building real wealth, then this chapter will really get you going. Why? Because what we're going to do now is, once and for all, get rid of that pain-in-the-neck thing called a budget.

I know what you're thinking.

Isn't the whole point of The Latte Factor to track how much I'm spending so I can figure out where to cut back? And doesn't that mean having a budget?

Nope. The point of The Latte Factor isn't to convince you to put yourself on a budget. It's to make you realize that you already earn enough to start saving and investing. Even better, that you already make enough to be rich.

IT'S TIME TO THROW OUT THE BUDGET

Now that you realize that almost everyone makes enough to become an Automatic Millionaire (you are realizing this, right?), it's time to address the next major misconception that holds most people back from achieving real wealth—the belief that the solution to this problem is budgeting.

Why do so many of us think we need a budget? Because that's what other people tell us. Probably someone told you, "Put yourself on a budget and everything will be fine." But who told you this? Your parents? A teacher? A spouse? A financial expert? I'm sure the people who gave you this advice were well intentioned. But were they rich? Were they happy and fun-loving? Were they successful budgeters themselves?

I doubt it.

VERY FEW OF US ARE BORN TO BUDGET

The fact is that very few of us are born to budget. And, truth be told, if we are "born budgeters," we inevitably fall in love with a born shopper! And our budget goes right out the window. Bam. See ya later, Mr. Budget.

If this describes your situation, don't worry. It's perfectly normal. Just about every couple I've ever met is like this. Unfortunately, if you like budgets and you marry a shopper, then no matter how much you love each other, you are going to fight about the money. The McIntyres fought about their budget and so did my wife, Michelle, and I when we first got married. (If you want to read a funny story about the first budget fight my wife and I had—it was the day we returned from our honeymoon—visit my web site at www.finishrich.com, where you can read the first chapter of *Smart Couples Finish Rich* for free.)

So what's the moral here? It's this . . .

THERE'S A BETTER WAY TO GET RICH THAN BUDGETING

There's a very simple reason why budgets don't work in the real world.

They aren't fun.

And because they're not fun, they are very difficult to stick to. Think about it. What budgeting boils down to is depriving yourself financially today for the sake of your future well-being. This is certainly a responsible idea, but as a strategy, it goes against human nature. Even worse, it goes against the 3,000 marketing messages that bombard you every day, urging you to spend every penny you earn.

I constantly hear so-called experts say things like, "You need to come up with a realistic budget for entertainment, eating out, clothing, housing, travel, food . . ." and on and on. That's just silly. It's right up there with telling people that the way to lose weight is to track every morsel they eat and count calories.

How many people do you know who went on a diet, became obsessed with counting calories and keeping track of how many grams of fat were in everything they ate (and everything *you* ate as well), and now seem to be even more overweight than ever? The reality is that these kinds of diets generally don't work. Why? Because most people get sick of counting calories. They get sick of depriving themselves.

The same thing happens with people on financial diets. For a while, they track every penny they spend. But then one day they can't take it anymore, and they go off on a shopping binge. There's no getting around it. Any system that is designed to control your normal human impulses is ultimately bound to fail.

That's because human beings don't want to be controlled. **We want to be *in* control.**

It's a huge difference. Believe me when I tell you that when it comes to money, you should control it. You should never let it control you. So take those budgets you've been struggling with and throw them in the garbage. If you really want to budget your expenses, that's your business, but I think it's a waste of time and effort. What I'm going to share with you instead is a system that allows you to stop worrying about budgeting once and for all. It's the system the McIntyres and every other Automatic Millionaire I know has used to get rich almost effortlessly.

My question to you is, are you ready for a simple approach?

IF THE ONLY THING YOU DID WAS THIS, YOU'D BE RICH

Bottom line. No exaggeration. No hype. If you want to be rich, all you have to do is make a decision to do something that most people don't do. And that's to PAY YOURSELF FIRST.

What most people do when they earn a dollar is pay everyone else first. They pay the landlord, the credit card company, the telephone company, the government, and on and on. The reason they think they need a budget is to help them figure out how much to pay everyone else so at the end of the month—or the year, or their working life—they will have something "left over" to pay themselves.

This, my friend, is absolutely, positively financially backwards. And because this system does not work, Americans wind up trying some pretty strange ways to get rich.

When you boil it down, there are basically six routes to wealth in this country. You can

- Win it
- Marry it
- Inherit it
- Sue for it
- Budget for it

OR

- Pay Yourself First.

Let's quickly review each of these methods.

Win it: Can you guess the number-one way average, hardworking people try to get rich in America? They play the lottery. Since 1964, when the New Hampshire Lottery made its debut (later to be joined by thirty-seven other states, the District of Columbia, Puerto Rico, and the U.S. Virgin Islands), Americans have plunked down more than $500 billion on lottery tickets. Can you imagine if these same dollars had been invested in retirement accounts? Now let me ask you something else. Have you ever won the lottery? Do you know anyone who has? Did that person share any winnings with you? Exactly. So let this one go.

Marry it: How's this working for you so far? There's a saying that it's as easy to marry a rich person as a poor one. Really? The truth is that people who marry for money generally end up paying for it for the rest of their lives. So let's skip this one too—unless, of course, you really do fall in love with someone who happens to have money.

Inherit it: This obviously isn't worth thinking about unless your parents are rich. And even if they are, isn't there something a little sick about visiting them during the holidays, asking how they are, and then thinking "bummer" when they say "I feel great"?

Sue for it: This one is really big these days. More than three quarters of the world's lawyers practice in the United States, and upwards of 94 percent of the world's lawsuits are filed here. It seems some people feel that rather than earn, save, and invest, a better strategy is find 'em, sue 'em, and sock it to 'em. In any case, it's not a real system that can be counted on to build wealth.

Budget for it: You can scrimp, brown bag it, clip coupons, track every penny you spend, never have fun, and put off living for thirty years in the hopeful expectation that someday you'll be able to retire and start enjoying your life. Yuck. That sounds terrible. No wonder this rarely works.

This leaves us with the one proven, *easy* way to get rich. And that is . . .

PAY YOURSELF FIRST

Chances are you've heard this phrase before. The idea that you should Pay Yourself First is not original, and it's certainly not new. I've been teaching it for years, and it had already been around for a long time when I started. As a rule, I always ask my students if they've heard of the Pay Yourself First concept. In virtually every single class or seminar I teach, whether there are five people in the room or five thousand, more than 90 percent raise their hands. (The other 10 percent have probably heard of it too, but they're the kind of people who aren't going to raise their hands no matter what I ask.)

But simply having heard of the concept doesn't mean you are living it. Before I explain in detail what this concept of Pay Yourself First means and how to use it, I want you to ask yourself the questions below and see if you know the answers. Even more important, see if you are living what you know.

DO YOU REALLY KNOW WHAT "PAY YOURSELF FIRST" MEANS?

- Do you know how much you should Pay Yourself First?
- Do you know where to put the money you Pay Yourself First?
- Are you actually doing it?
- Is your Pay Yourself First plan AUTOMATIC?

Based on how people answer these questions, I can tell immediately if they have a realistic plan to become rich. The truth is that most people don't.

So how did you just do? Are you Paying Yourself First? Do you know what percentage you are Paying Yourself First? Are you putting the money in the right place? Is your Pay Yourself First plan automatic so that you don't have to budget, or write checks manually—or even think about it—in order to save?

If you can answer all these questions with an unequivocal "yes," congratulations. You are truly amazing. You are doing more than most people ever will to attain financial freedom. But keep reading just the same, because this book contains ideas that a take-action person like you can use to get to the next level.

On the other hand, if your answer to some or all of the questions is "no," don't beat yourself up. You're perfectly normal. **Most people don't pay themselves first; nor do they have an automatic plan**. Most people are only hoping to get rich. And hoping never works. Sure, maybe these people could get rich by accident. They could win the lottery. Or they could get hit by a bus and sue the city for a million dollars. But this isn't a plan.

And you want a plan.

So if you can't answer all those questions in the affirmative, don't worry. The rest of this book will show you how to get it right.

WHAT "PAY YOURSELF FIRST" MEANS

Pay Yourself First means just what it says. When you earn a dollar, the first person you pay is you. Most people don't do this. When most people earn a dollar, the first person they pay is Uncle Sam. They earn a dollar, and before it even makes it onto their paycheck, they pay the government something like 27 cents in federal income withholding taxes (often more). Then, depending on which state they live in, they may pay an average of 5 more cents in state income tax. On top of that, there are Social Security taxes, Medicare, and unemployment. In the end, they wind up paying the government first as much as 35 or 40 cents of their hard-earned dollar. *Seems like everyone is getting paid but the person who earned the paycheck.*

IT WASN'T ALWAYS LIKE THIS

The government didn't always grab a chunk of your paycheck before you even saw it. Up until 1943, people got their money when they earned it, and they weren't asked to pay income taxes until the next spring. From the government's point of view, however, there was a problem with this system. People just couldn't be counted on to budget well enough to have enough money in reserve to be able to pay their taxes the following spring when the bill came due.

Think about that for a second. The government is pretty smart. It figured out years ago that people couldn't budget, so it set up a system to make sure it got "paid first." Not only did the government arrange to get paid first, it *automated the process* so there wouldn't be any slip-ups. It figured out a darn near foolproof way to make sure it would always get its money. No ifs, ands, or buts.

This fact is crucially important. It's so crucial that I'd like you to read the last two paragraphs over again and then really think about what they mean. If you do, the rest of this book is going to be a no-brainer. That's because what you're going to do is exactly what the government figured out it needed to do to keep the cash rolling in. It came up with a system that would always work with regular people—a system that is based on the way people really are, rather than the way they think they should be. It's actually kind of brilliant. Now you need to do the same thing. **You need to set up a system that guarantees you'll get paid—a system in which you Pay Yourself First AUTOMATICALLY.**

The good news is that you can and it's easy.

DON'T PAY THE GOVERNMENT FIRST

If there was a legal way to avoid it, why on earth would you allow the government to have first crack at your paycheck? Remember, Uncle Sam's cut totals roughly 30 cents of every dollar you make. That leaves you with just 70 cents to spend on EVERYTHING ELSE, including retirement savings and investing. Talk about tough. That's income shrinkage if I've ever seen it.

This is why so many people have trouble making ends meet. Say your salary is $50,000 a year. (This is a bit more than the average person earns, but let's use it as a base to keep the math simple.) Since you're paying the government first, you're not really earning $50,000. What you're actually earning is about 70 percent of $50,000—or $35,000. That's all the money you really have to pay your bills and try to build up a nest egg. Not very much, is it? No wonder so many people think they need to be on a budget.

THE SECRET IS THE WAY YOUR MONEY FLOWS

You have a right to legally avoid federal and state taxes on the money you earn. The key word is "legally." You can legally Pay Yourself First, instead of the government, simply by using what is called a pretax retirement account. There are many different types of these accounts, with names like 401(k) or

403(b) plans, IRAs, and SEP IRAs. We'll cover them in detail later on.

HOW MUCH SHOULD I PAY MYSELF FIRST?

The most often asked question about Pay Yourself First is "How much?" There's a simple answer to the question, but in order to make it really clear, let me tell you a story.

WHO YOU WORK FOR IS WAITING FOR YOU AT HOME

While driving home on the freeway not too long ago, I saw a billboard that said, "Who you work for is waiting for you at home." At first, it made me laugh. Then it made me think.

As much as our employers would like us to believe otherwise, the reason most of us go to work each morning isn't the company mission statement or even serving the customer. It's ultimately about us. When it comes down to it, the reason most of us go to work is for the sake of ourselves and our families. We go to work to protect those we love. Everything else is secondary. We are our first priority.

Or are we? The truth is that we are not raised to put ourselves first. We are raised to be nice. We are raised to share. We are raised to help others.

These are wonderful values, and I believe in them. But

there's something else I also believe: the old saying that the Lord helps those who help themselves. I think there is timeless truth in this. So before we start laying out a financial plan, let's really focus on these questions: Are we helping ourselves? Are you helping yourself? Are you REALLY working for yourself?

I'm not asking if you're self-employed. I'm asking whether you're really working for your own benefit and that of your family when you go to your job each morning.

HOW MANY HOURS DID YOU WORK LAST WEEK?

Do the math. Fill in the blanks below to figure out whom you're really working for.

LAST WEEK, I WORKED A TOTAL OF _____ HOURS.

I EARN $_____ AN HOUR (BEFORE TAXES).

LAST WEEK, I PUT ASIDE $_____ FOR MY
RETIREMENT.

SO LAST WEEK, I WORKED _____ HOURS FOR
MYSELF.

Did that last sentence stump you? Are you asking yourself: "What does he mean—how many hours did I work for myself last week?"

It's actually pretty simple. To figure out how many hours you worked for yourself last week, you first need to ask yourself how much money you saved last week. If your answer is zero, then you worked zero hours for yourself last week. If, however, you did save something last week, then divide the amount of money you put aside for your retirement last week by your hourly income. For example, if your income before taxes (also called your "pretax" or "gross" income) averages $25 an hour and you put aside $50 last week, you would divide $50 by $25, which gives you two—meaning you worked two hours for yourself last week.

The answer you got can tell you a lot about the kind of future you can expect to have. I know from experience that most people work less than one hour a week for themselves. And that's not nearly enough.

Let's consider someone who earns $50,000 a year.

A PERSON WHO EARNS $50,000 A YEAR . . .

. . . earns roughly $1,000 a week (figuring two weeks off for vacation)

. . . or roughly $25 an hour (for a 40-hour week).

So how much should he or she be saving each week?

As we've already seen (and as the McIntyres' experience has shown us), a good savings benchmark to shoot for is between 10 percent and 15 percent of your gross income. To keep it simple, let's split the difference and call it 12.5 percent. Now 12.5 percent of $1,000 is $125—meaning that if you're earning a gross income of $1,000 a week, you should be saving $125 a week. Figuring a five-day workweek, that comes to $25 a day.

In other words, you should be saving the equivalent of one hour's worth of income each day.

Unfortunately, most people don't even come close to saving that much. According to the U.S. Department of Commerce, the average American saves well below 5 percent of what he or she earns. In other words, **most of us work barely 22 minutes a day for ourselves.** And one out of five workers don't put in any time at all for themselves—meaning they don't save anything.

YOU COULD BE WORKING FOR YOUR FUTURE

I find this truly sad. Why would you get out of bed, leave your family, spend most of your waking hours taking care of business for someone else, and NOT work at least one hour a day for yourself? The answer is you shouldn't. And starting today, I hope you won't.

What I've just described should really get you thinking. It might even get you mad. You might be thinking right now, "You know, this is crazy. I really should be working more hours for me. Why wouldn't I work an hour a day for me? Why wouldn't I work an *hour and a half* for me? Why not *two hours* a day for me?"

The problem with most financial planning and financial education is that it focuses on numbers and not on people's lives. Instead of thinking just about percentages of income, think about hours of your life. How many hours were you planning on working for yourself this year, instead of for your employer, the government, the credit card companies, the bank, and everyone else who wants a piece of what you earn? How many hours of this week do you think your future is worth? What about today? **How many hours do you want to spend today working for your future?**

It seems to me that an hour a day is really not so much to ask in return for a bright future. If you're not saving that much of your income right now, you are working too much for others and not enough for yourself. You deserve better.

SO LET'S GET STARTED

My suggestion is simple. Starting today, you should work at least one hour a day for yourself. This means you should Pay Yourself First for your future by putting a minimum of 10 percent of your gross income into what we call a pretax retirement account.

Here is all you need to do (details on how to do this follow in the next chapter).

- Decide to Pay Yourself First for your future.
- Open a retirement account.
- Fund it with 10 percent of your gross income.
- **Make It Automatic.**

STARTING TODAY,
I'M WORKING FOR ME

You can think about this a little longer, or you can commit to yourself now to make it happen. Here's a way to ensure that you take action. From years of firsthand experience meeting the readers of my books at my seminars, I've learned that people who write out their goals and plans generally wind up accomplishing a lot more than people who don't. So with this in mind, please go find a pen and fill out the following commitment to yourself. Do it today, this minute, RIGHT NOW.

THE AUTOMATIC MILLIONAIRE PROMISE

I, _____ [insert name], hereby promise myself that starting this week I will work at least one hour a day for myself because I deserve it.

Therefore, I promise that I will start Paying Myself First ____% of my gross income no later than ____ [insert date].

Signed: _____

THERE IS NO CATCH!

Let's say that tomorrow you started having 10 percent of your gross income, before taxes, automatically taken out of your paycheck and put in a pretax retirement account. (Don't worry how; we'll get to that soon enough.) As a result of that simple, automatic process, you would eventually accumulate more wealth than 90 percent of the population. That's right. Paying Yourself First just 10 percent of your income can help you achieve enormous wealth.

What's the catch? Well, for some people, it's the idea of not having that 10 percent to spend. But how difficult is that, really? Think back to The Latte Factor. Let's once again use the example of someone who makes $50,000 a year. If that's your annual salary and you took 10 percent out of each paycheck before the government got its bite, by the end of the year, you'd have put aside $5,000.

Now, if you hadn't put anything aside over the course of the year but instead waited until December to come up with this much money, how likely is it that you'd have $5,000 sitting around somewhere? Not very. But when you Pay Yourself First, you don't wait. The 10 percent is taken out of your paycheck and automatically invested for you before you ever see it. You can't spend what you don't have, right?

So how much would this cost you day by day?

Let's see. An annual income of $50,000 equals about $4,200 a month. That's just over $2,000 every two weeks (which is how most people are paid). So to save 10 percent of that, you'd have to put aside about $200 every two weeks—or $14 a day.

Now, let's ask how much it will cost you if you don't Pay Yourself First. If you invested just $200 every two weeks for 35 years in a retirement account that earned an annual return of 10 percent, what would you have?

The answer is that you would have more than 1 million dollars. Actually, a *lot* more.

The exact figure is $1,678,293.78.

That's what it costs you if you *don't* Pay Yourself First.

WHY THIS WON'T HURT

Some people will read this and say, "Put aside fourteen dollars a day! Is he nuts? There's no way I could save fourteen dollars a day."

If you're one of these people, don't worry. It's a perfectly normal reaction. Just keep reading.

In the next chapter, you'll see how it's actually easier and far more painless than you might think to save that much. For you impatient types, here's a sneak peek at the explanation: If you put the money into a pretax retirement account (something you'll learn about in a few more pages), saving $14 a day actually reduces your spendable income by only about $10 a day. Don't worry if this doesn't seem to make sense. The next chapter will make it all crystal clear.

THE "PAY YOURSELF FIRST" FORMULA

Over the years, I've received a tremendous number of e-mail messages asking me for a Pay Yourself First formula. "Is 10 percent enough?" people will ask. "I heard I should save 12 percent. What about more? What happens if I save 15 percent of my income?"

So here's the formula I use now. Everyone's life is different, but this should give you a benchmark to shoot for or plan around.

To be . . .

Dead Broke: Don't Pay Yourself First. Spend more than you make. Borrow money on credit cards and carry debt you can't pay off.

Poor: Think about Paying Yourself First, but don't actually do it. Spend everything you make each month and save nothing. Keep telling yourself, "Someday . . ."

Middle Class: Pay Yourself First 5 to 10 percent of your gross income.

Upper Middle Class: Pay Yourself First 10 to 15 percent of your gross income.

Rich: Pay Yourself First 15 to 20 percent of your gross income.

Rich Enough to Retire Early: Pay Yourself First at least 20 percent of your gross income.

IS THAT ALL THERE IS?

To be honest, not everyone is as enthralled by the idea of Pay Yourself First as they should be. In fact, it makes a lot of people angry. You may be one of them. Your head may be full of reasons why you can't Pay Yourself First. You may be thinking right now, "I need more than this. Where's the secret to wealth? Where's the stock or mutual fund investment that will take care of me? How do I earn 10 percent a year by investing? Aren't those days gone? How do I buy real estate with no money down? That's the kind of advice that I need."

Please trust me on this. Nothing will help you achieve wealth until you decide to Pay Yourself First. Nothing. You can read every book, listen to every tape program, order every motivational product, subscribe to every newsletter there is, and none of it will get you anywhere if you let the government and everyone else have first crack at your paycheck before you get to it. **The foundation of wealth building is Pay Yourself First.**

On page 73, you committed to Paying Yourself First. Now, you must decide two things.

1. HOW will you do it?
2. WHERE will you put the money?

The next chapter is devoted to answering those questions. So let's go. Your thinking has changed. Now let's look at changing the way you act. You are ready to become an Automatic Millionaire.

AUTOMATIC MILLIONAIRE ACTION STEPS

If you get only one message from this book, it should be this: **The secret to creating lasting financial change is to decide to Pay Yourself First and then Make It Automatic.** If all you do are these two things, you will never have to worry about money again.

Sound simple? That's because it is.

Reviewing the steps we laid out in this chapter, here's what you should be doing right now to become an Automatic Millionaire. (Once again, check off each step as you accomplish it.)

❑ Forget about budgeting.

❑ Forget about get-rich-quick schemes.

❑ Make the commitment to Pay Yourself First.

❑ Decide whether you want to be poor, middle class, or rich, and choose the right percentage to Pay Yourself First.

Now turn the page and learn how to Make It Automatic.

CHAPTER FOUR

NOW

MAKE

IT

AUTOMATIC

Maybe you've heard all this before and you already know what *not* Paying Yourself First costs you. Having this knowledge hasn't changed your life before, so why should anything be different now? Well, the difference is, this time you're going to take control. This time you're going to Make It Automatic.

There's no getting around it. In order for Pay Yourself First to be effective, **the process has to be automatic.** Whatever you decide to do with the money you're paying yourself— whether you intend to park it in a retirement account, save it as a security blanket, invest it in a college fund, put it aside to help you buy a home, or use it to pay down your mortgage or credit card debt—**you need to have a system that doesn't depend on your following a budget or being disciplined.**

Having worked with clients as a financial advisor for many years, I can tell you that the only plans that work are the ones that are automatic. Clients would tell me all the time, "David, I'm super-disciplined. I'll write the checks each month and mail them to you to invest." It never lasted. Most people paid themselves first this way for maybe three months. A few made it to six months. In nine years, I had only one client who manually wrote his checks and was disciplined enough to stick to it.

HOW THE AUTOMATIC
MILLIONAIRES DID IT

Jim and Sue McIntyre became Automatic Millionaires by setting up a Pay Yourself First system that automatically arranged for them to save upwards of 10 percent of their income, month in and month out, for more than thirty years. This doesn't mean they started at 10 percent. At the very beginning, they paid themselves only 4 percent of their income. Then they bumped it up to 5 percent. After another year went by, they increased it to 7 percent. It took them four years to get to 10 percent. A few years later, they decided to really go for it, and so they increased the amount to 15 percent.

What made all this possible was the fact that they never had to write any checks themselves. Because their plan was automatic, it didn't take any discipline on their part. It didn't take time. It didn't even take a lot of thinking. In fact, the only decision they had to make was how big a percentage of their paychecks they wanted to Pay Themselves First. They did it once. The rest was automatic.

Like the McIntyres, I also started gradually. When I first heard about this concept I was doing what most people do—trying to budget, beating up on myself for failing, and then scrambling at the end of the year to find some money to put in my retirement and savings accounts, only to find another year had come and gone and I had not made any financial progress.

I actually started by Paying Myself First just 1 percent of my income. That's right—only 1 percent. I was in my mid-twenties, and I wanted to make sure it didn't hurt. Within three months, I realized that 1 percent was easy, so I increased the amount to 3 percent.

It was around then that I met the McIntyres and said to myself, "Enough is enough—I want to start young and finish rich."

After our meeting, I made a phone call and increased my percentage to 10 percent. A year later, I bumped it up again to 15 percent. Today, my wife, Michelle, and I each strive to pay ourselves the first 20 percent of our gross income. That may sound like a lot, but because I've worked up to it gradually over the course of fifteen years, it's become our "new normal."

I'm not sharing my story to brag. I'm sharing it because if you are not Paying Yourself First now, that's probably because you think you can't afford to, and I know just how that feels.

I used to feel that way myself. But I can tell you from personal experience that once you decide to Pay Yourself First and then you Make It Automatic, it's done—and within the first three months, you totally forget about it. You'd be amazed how effortlessly you can learn to live on a little less. And it becomes easier as you go along. Why? Because before you know it, you have thousands and thousands of dollars in savings. What makes this possible is very simple: You can't spend what you don't have in your pocket.

So even if you think the most you could part with right now is just 1 percent of your gross income, that's okay—go ahead and get started. This one little step will change your habits and make saving automatic. And that will put you on a path that ultimately will make you rich.

YOUR FIRST PRIORITY: BUYING YOURSELF A SECURE FUTURE

I know by now you are motivated to act. You've found your Latte Factor. You've looked at how many hours a week you currently work for yourself. And you've committed on paper to work at least one hour a day for yourself. Now it's time to get the Automatic Millionaire future you want. So let's go get it.

How do you get a secure financial future? It's simple. You buy it. You decide today that you won't ever be financially dependent on the government, your employer, or even your family to enjoy a stress-free life after retirement. You are going to be one of those people who get to do what they want to do when they want to do it.

The way you accomplish this is by committing yourself to invest the money you've decided to Pay Yourself First *in your future*. Paying Yourself First for your future is the Automatic Millionaire's first priority. It involves setting up a system that will automatically fund your own personal retirement account. Over the next few pages, I will explain exactly how you can do this.

IF YOU HAVE A RETIREMENT PLAN AT WORK, USE IT!

If you are an employee, I have great news for you: The chances are excellent that what follows will be EASY. I say this because hundreds of thousands of companies in the United States offer employees what are called self-directed retirement accounts. These plans allow you to contribute your own money to your own personal retirement account *without paying taxes on it*.

The most common self-directed retirement account is known as a 401(k) plan. The 401(k) is considered to be the mother of all retirement accounts. If you work for a non-profit organization such as a school or a hospital, you will likely be offered a similar plan called a 403(b) plan. (The numbers and letters refer to the parts of the tax code that established these various retirement plans.) In essence, both plans offer the same opportunities.

There are six key reasons why you shouldn't pass up the chance to enroll in one of these plans if you are eligible.

- You don't pay any income tax on the money you put into the plan or on any of the returns it earns for you over the years—not a cent in taxes until you take it out.
- As of 2006, you can put in as much as $15,000 a year (more if you are over age fifty and more in future years; see page 92 for details).
- You can arrange things so that your contributions are handled automatically through payroll deduction.
- It's free (most employers offer these plans to employees without charge).
- You may even get FREE MONEY from your employer (many companies offer to match a percentage of employee contributions).
- By contributing to your plan from every paycheck, you can enjoy the miraculous benefits of compound interest.

THE POWER OF GETTING PAID
BEFORE THE GOVERNMENT

As we noted in the last chapter, the government normally grabs about 30 cents from every dollar you earn before you ever even see the money, leaving you with only about 70 cents. But when you make a contribution to a tax-deferred retirement plan, you get to do so with the entire dollar. It's now the government that gets bypassed. This is what gives tax-deferred investments such a terrific advantage over regular investments. The following table shows just how terrific they are.

THE POWER OF PRETAX INVESTING

	401(k) Retirement Plan (Pretax)	Regular Investment (Taxable)
Gross income	$1.00	$1.00
Minus taxes	-0	-30%
Amount available to invest	$1.00	$0.70
Plus annual return	+ 10%	+ 10%
Balance after one year	**$1.10**	**$0.77**
Are gains taxable?	No	Yes

THE POWER OF EMPLOYER MATCHING

	401(k) Retirement Plan (Pretax with Employer Match)	Regular Investment (Taxable)
Gross income	$1.00	$1.00
Minus taxes	-0	-30%
Amount available to invest	$1.00	$0.70
Typical employer match	+25%	0
Amount invested	$1.25	$0.70
Plus annual return	+10%	+10%
Balance after one year	**$1.38**	**$0.77**
Are gains taxable?	No	Yes

How much would you rather have after a year— $1.10 or 77 cents? This a no-brainer. But wait—it might get better. Many companies offer to match a percentage of employee retirement contributions. If yours is one of them, you could come out really far ahead.

Think about it—$1.38 vs. 77 cents. You get almost a 100 percent increase in your net savings simply by using a pretax retirement account! That's huge—and it's only year one.

Look at the chart on page 87 to see what happens if you do this over time, with real money.

GET IN THE GAME

Pretax retirement plans are where all wealth starts. Yet according to a November 2002 survey by PlanSponsor.com, one out of every four American workers who are eligible for retirement accounts hasn't even bothered to sign up. When it comes to assuring their futures, these people are not even in the game. They are watching from the sidelines. If you are one of them, consider today your sign-up day. When you finish reading this chapter, I want you to telephone the benefits office at your company and ask them to provide you with what they probably call their retirement enrollment kit. If your employer is a large company, you may be able to access this material online through the company web site.

Many people mistakenly assume that if their company offers employees a 401(k) or 403(b) retirement plan, they are automatically included in it. THIS IS ALMOST NEVER THE

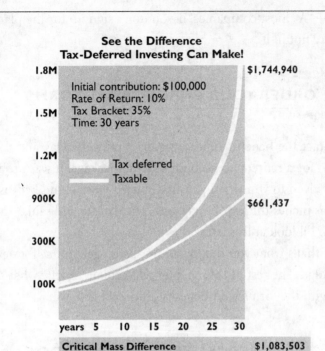

**See the Difference
Tax-Deferred Investing Can Make!**

Initial contribution: $100,000
Rate of Return: 10%
Tax Bracket: 35%
Time: 30 years

$1,744,940

Tax deferred
Taxable

$661,437

years 5   10   15   20   25   30

| Critical Mass Difference | $1,083,503 |

Tax deferral can grow more money.

Turning Growth into Income

From	Taxable	Tax Deferred
Accumulation	$661,437	$1,744,940
Rate of Return	at 10%	at 10%
Annual Earnings	$66,143	$174,494
Tax Bracket	at 35%	at 35%
Annual Income	**$42,993**	**$113,422**

Tax-deferred growth can lead to more income.

CASE. At most companies, if you don't sign up for the plan, you're not in it.

ORDER YOUR ENROLLMENT FORMS

Contact the benefits office at your employer today and ask them for a retirement account sign-up package. It was probably given to you when you first started work—and because it was inches thick, you may have put it aside and said, "Too busy. I'll look at this later."

If that's what you did, by all means go get yourself a new package. The rest of this chapter will explain exactly what to do with the forms your benefits office will give you.

PICK A PERCENTAGE . . . THEN DO A LITTLE MORE

Now that you have your sign-up package, you need to decide what percentage of your income you're going to funnel into your retirement account every pay period. In the sign-up package, you'll find a form for you to sign authorizing your employer to deduct money from your paycheck to fund your retirement account. Most plans will ask you whether you want the amount deducted from your paycheck to be a set percentage of your income or a specific dollar amount. If you have a choice, *always select a percentage.* That way, when you get a raise and your salary increases, the amount you're putting into your retirement account will automatically increase along with it.

As we've already discussed, you should ideally try to save at least one hour's worth of your income each day. On a percentage basis, that would come to roughly 10 percent of your gross income.

We've also discussed the fact that it's okay to start off slowly, saving a smaller percentage of your income at first and gently working your way up to where you need to be. So as I said before, even if you think the best you can do is to save just 1 percent, don't let that stop you. Anything is better than nothing.

At the same time, try to be ambitious. After all, this is your future we're talking about. However much you think you can afford to Pay Yourself First for your future—do more. If you think you can save 4 percent save 6 percent. If you think you can save 10 percent, save 12 percent. Most of us tend to underestimate how much we think we can manage. As a result, we wind up low-balling ourselves . . . and our future.

IT'S EASIER THAN YOU THINK

In fact, the actual pinch almost always turns out to be less painful than you'd think. To understand why this is so, consider the story Jim and Sue McIntyre told me about their eldest daughter, Donna, and her husband, Mark. Inspired by her parents' example of Paying Yourself First, Donna decided she and Mark should put 10 percent of their gross earnings into a pretax retirement account. Since the two of them had an annual income of about $50,000, that meant putting aside $5,000 a year.

Mark certainly liked the idea of having a secure future, but he thought Donna's plan was crazy. "We're living paycheck to paycheck," he told her. "There's no way we can afford to save $5,000 a year. That would be like taking a $5,000-a-year pay cut."

"But we don't have to take a $5,000 pay cut," Donna replied. "That's the beauty of pretax investing."

"You're telling me we can save $5,000 a year without giving ourselves a $5,000 pay cut?" Mark asked.

"That's right," Donna said.

Mark rolled his eyes. "This I gotta hear."

It took Donna a while to explain it to him, but by the time she was finished, Mark was willing to give it a try. I hope you will be too. Here's what she told him.

"Normally we earn around $50,000 a year, right?"

Mark nodded.

"Wrong. We've got a combined tax rate of around 30 percent, which means we actually bring home only about $35,000 in spendable income. Now, I bet you think that paying ourselves first $5,000 a year will reduce that $35,000 to $30,000."

Mark nodded again, though this time with a bit less conviction.

"Wrong again. Remember, we're paying ourselves first—*before* we pay the government. In other words, the $5,000 we're saving comes off the top. What gets reduced is our gross income, which will drop from $50,000 to $45,000."

"But that's still $5,000," Mark protested.

"We're not done yet," Donna said. "Let's do the math: $45,000 taxed at 30 percent leaves the two of us with a spendable income of $31,500. Before, we had a net spendable income of $35,000. Now we're getting $31,500. The difference is $3,500 a year. NOT $5,000."

Mark stared at her for a long minute, working it out in his head. "Pretty cool," he said finally. "We save $5,000, but our income goes down by only $3,500."

"That's right," Donna agreed. "And you know how little $3,500 is? Between the two of us, it's about $290 a month. That's only $145 a month each. That's less than $5 a day. I think we can handle that, don't you?"

In fact, Donna and Mark stopped noticing the difference in their take-home pay within a few months. And their experience was absolutely typical. I promise you—once you start Paying Yourself First, within a month, you'll have totally gotten used to it. The only difference you'll notice is how good you're feeling knowing that you are now on track to be an Automatic Millionaire. This one change to your financial life will ultimately change your financial destiny.

NOW MAX IT OUT

If you are already enrolled in your company's retirement plan, congratulations. But that doesn't mean you're done yet. Now you need to find out how much you are using it. Are you saving 4 percent? That's about what most people do. Unfor-

tunately, most people retire poor, dependent on Social Security or family to survive. You are not most people.

In a perfect world, the fastest way to become rich is to
MAX OUT THE PLAN. This means making what your employer tells you is the largest contribution you can make under your plan's rules. Here's the maximum allowable based
on current tax law:

401(K), 403(B), AND 457 PLAN CONTRIBUTION LIMITS		
Year	Maximum Allowable (if age 49 or younger)	Maximum Allowable (if age 50 or older)
2002	$11,000	$12,000
2003	$12,000	$14,000
2004	$13,000	$16,000
2005	$14,000	$18,000
2006	$15,000	$20,000

Note: After 2006, increases will be adjusted for inflation in $500
increments.

While you can use this table as a guide, you should still
check with your employer's benefits office. If your company
has a poor participation rate (meaning your fellow workers
are not Paying Themselves First), then your maximum allowable contribution may be lower. So don't guess at this. Check
with your benefits office *today*. And recheck the maximums
every January, so you can take full advantage of any increases
that may have been made.

THE SINGLE BIGGEST INVESTMENT MISTAKE YOU CAN MAKE

The single most important investment decision you ever make may well be how much to automatically Pay Yourself First into your retirement account. Other than buying a home (something we will cover later), this one decision can do more than any other action you may take in your life to determine whether or not you will become rich.

With this in mind, it shouldn't be hard to figure out the single biggest investment mistake you can make: not using your plan and not maxing it out.

People who aren't serious about being rich say this:
- "I can't afford to save more than 4 percent of my income."
- "My spouse is enrolled in his/her plan, so I don't need to enroll in mine."
- "Our plan isn't any good, so it's not worth using."
- "My company doesn't match retirement contributions, so signing up for the plan isn't worth it."
- "Investing in stocks is foolish."
- "I'll save more later."

Serious wealth builders say this:
- "No matter what, I will Pay Myself First."
- "I will Pay Myself First at least 10 percent of my income and strive to contribute the maximum amount I'm allowed to my retirement account."

- "I will make sure my spouse is doing the same."
- "I understand that when the stock market goes down, it allows me to buy stocks at bargain prices . . . and that's a good thing."
- **"I know the time to save for tomorrow is always today!"**

JIM AND SUE'S FRIENDS: A $500,000 DIFFERENCE!

If you think I'm being a broken record here, going on about the importance of maxing out your retirement plan, consider this story Jim and Sue McIntyre told me about two couples they were friendly with. The story impressed me so much that I've been retelling it for years.

The first couple, Marilyn and Robert, had spent thirty years focusing their retirement efforts on funding Robert's retirement account at work. When Robert's employer, an oil company, first began offering a 401(k) plan that would allow workers to put away as much as 15 percent of their income, Robert and Marilyn figured it made sense for Robert to participate, but they weren't sure they could afford to put so much of Robert's paycheck aside. In the end, Jim McIntyre put it in perspective. "Robert," he said, "the two of you *can't* afford not to do this. Just make the sacrifice now, and you'll be very glad later on that you did." With that sensible advice ringing in his ears, Robert elected to make the maximum contribution of 15 percent.

SOMEDAY NEVER CAME

At the same time, Robert and Marilyn's best friends, Larry and Connie, were wrestling with the same issues. Larry had a job very similar to Robert's, and the two men earned roughly the same amount of money. But Larry and Connie made a different decision. After a great deal of discussion, they decided to put away just 6 percent of Larry's income. They simply didn't feel they could afford to put away any more than that. They thought they would get around to increasing the percentage sometime down the road . . . when things got easier.

Twenty fast years later, when Robert and Larry were in their fifties, they were both downsized. For Robert and Marilyn, it wasn't really a problem. They were ready to retire anyway and they knew they had saved enough to be able to do it comfortably. Indeed, as a result of maxing out his contributions, Robert had more than $935,000 in his 401(k) account.

Larry and Connie weren't in such good shape. Larry never did get around to increasing his percentage and had only about $450,000 in his 401(k) account—almost $500,000 less than Robert. He and Connie were still able to retire, but from then on their lives were not nearly as comfortable as Robert and Marilyn's.

Learn from Larry and Connie's example. Don't make the same mistake they did. Maximize your retirement contribution now. *Take just this one action and you will have changed your financial future for the better—guaranteed.*

AUTOMATION PLUS COMPOUND INTEREST EQUALS SERIOUS WEALTH

Beyond the tax breaks, beyond the "free money" you can get from an employer who matches contributions, the single biggest reason why Paying Yourself First into a retirement account at work is such an effective way to build wealth is that you **Make It Automatic.** Once you sign up at the benefits office, that's it. You don't have to do anything. Your contributions are automatically deducted from your paycheck and automatically put in your retirement account. Because this process is automatic, the chances are pretty good that you will continue doing it for a long time. And by doing that, you will get to enjoy the benefits of a mathematical phenomenon most people don't really understand but everyone can use to become rich—the miracle of compound interest.

It comes down to this:

Over time, money compounds.
Over a lot of time, money compounds dramatically!

You don't have to take my word for this. Consider the following table, which illustrates how the miracle of compounding can transform a relatively small but consistent amount of saving into major wealth. It shows how much money you can make by depositing $100 a month over varying periods of time at varying interest rates.

Do you see what compounding does? Over a forty-year

SAVINGS GROWTH OF $100 DEPOSITED MONTHLY

Depending on the rate of return, putting just $100 a month into an
interest-bearing account and then letting it compound
can generate a surprisingly large nest egg

Interest Rate	5 Years	10 Years	15 Years	20 Years	25 Years	30 Years	35 Years	40 Years
$100/mo invested at 2.0%	$6,315	$13,294	$21,006	$29,529	$38,947	$49,355	$60,856	$73,566
$100/mo invested at 3.0%	6,481	14,009	22,754	32,912	44,712	58,419	74,342	92,837
$100/mo invested at 4.0%	6,652	14,774	24,691	36,800	51,584	69,636	91,678	118,590
$100/mo invested at 5.0%	6,829	15,593	26,840	41,275	59,799	83,573	114,083	153,238
$100/mo invested at 6.0%	7,012	16,470	29,227	49,435	69,646	100,954	143,183	200,145
$100/mo invested at 7.0%	7,201	17,409	31,881	52,397	81,480	122,709	181,156	264,012
$100/mo invested at 8.0%	7,397	18,417	34,835	59,295	95,737	150,030	230,918	351,428
$100/mo invested at 9.0%	7,599	19,497	38,124	67,290	112,953	184,447	296,385	471,643
$100/mo invested at 10.0%	7,808	20,655	41,792	76,570	133,789	227,933	382,828	637,678
$100/mo invested at 11.0%	8,025	21,899	45,886	87,357	159,058	283,023	497,347	867,896
$100/mo invested at 12.0%	8,249	23,234	50,458	99,915	189,764	352,991	649,527	1,188,242

span, a $100-a-month savings program costs you a total of $48,000. Yet at even moderate rates of return (say, 6 percent a year), you wind up with $200,145—more than four times the amount you actually put in. And at the higher rate (12 percent), you come out with a nest egg worth nearly *25 times* your total contribution.

WHAT IF YOU DON'T HAVE A COMPANY RETIREMENT PLAN?

First, don't give up. The fact that your employer doesn't offer a retirement plan doesn't mean you'll never be rich. It simply means that in order to become rich you will have to be a bit more proactive. But don't worry. It shouldn't take you more than an hour to do what needs to be done. And what's one hour? Compared to the time most of us spend watching television each week, it's nothing. But it could change your life.

THIS WEEK, OPEN AN INDIVIDUAL RETIREMENT ACCOUNT

An IRA—or Individual Retirement Account—is a personal retirement plan that most anyone who earns an income can set up at a bank, a brokerage firm, or even online. Like a 401(k) or 403(b) plan, an IRA is not an investment itself. Rather, it's a financial holding tank into which you can make tax-deferred contributions of up to $4,000 a year ($4,500 a year if you are age fifty or older) with your Pay Yourself First dollars. When you open an IRA, you first decide how much to put in, then how to invest it. (Many people invest their IRA money in a mutual fund. More on this later.)

There are currently two types of IRAs that you should consider: the traditional IRA and the Roth IRA. Read on and you'll find out why.

THE TRADITIONAL IRA VS. THE ROTH IRA

The biggest difference between a traditional IRA and a Roth IRA involves when you pay income tax on your retirement money.

With a traditional IRA, you contribute pretax dollars.[1] But while you don't pay any income tax on the money you put into the account, you are liable for income tax on any money you withdraw. And you are required to withdraw your money by the time you reach the age of 70½.

The opposite is true of Roth IRAs. You do pay income tax on the money you put in. (In other words, your contributions aren't deductible.) And there are income limits on who can use a Roth IRA.[2] The good news about Roth IRAs is that as long as your money has been in the account for at least five

---

[1] A traditional IRA may not be tax deductible if you are covered by an employer plan. Check IRS Publication #590, for details.

[2] If you earn less than $95,000 a year ($150,000 for married couples), you can contribute up to $4,000 a year. If you earn more than that, the amount you can put in is reduced. If your earnings top $110,000 a year ($160,000 for married couples), you can't use a Roth IRA at all.

years and you are older than 59½, there's no tax to pay when you take it out. And unlike the traditional IRA, you are not forced by the government to start taking money out at age 70½.

HOW DO I DECIDE?

The choice on whether to go with an IRA or a Roth IRA really boils down to the question of whether you want your tax breaks up front or later on.

Many experts say it's always better to take advantage of the kind of up-front tax deductions you get with a traditional IRA. Other experts prefer the Roth IRA because once you reach retirement age, it can provide you with tax-free income for the rest of your life. So which is better—up front or later on? In the end, it depends on what tax bracket you'll be in when you retire, and that's something you really can't know for sure. Common sense would tell you that you'll probably be in a lower tax bracket, since you won't be working anymore. But who knows what the tax laws will be then? According to most computer projections, if you are at least fifteen years away from when you plan to begin withdrawing money from your retirement account, you'd probably do better with a Roth IRA. Still, without knowing your personal situation, it's hard to say *exactly* which plan may make the most sense for you.

I happen to like the traditional IRA account because the tax deduction makes it easier for you to max it out. In order for you to contribute $3,000 to a Roth IRA, you really need to save closer to $4,000 because you have to pay taxes on your earnings before you can use them to make your contribution. However, if you think you can buckle down and save enough to fully fund a Roth IRA—and you're more than fifteen years away from retirement—then the Roth IRA is a great choice because when you retire all the money you take out of this account will be tax free! Also, if you can't get a tax deduction on the traditional IRA because you are covered by an employer plan, don't even consider doing a traditional IRA. Go with the Roth IRA.

For more information visit www.rothira.com. This is a great web site that covers the comparison issues between Roth and traditional IRAs, and also offers links to many articles and other sites that address the subject in detail.

MAKING YOUR IRA AUTOMATIC

Many people underestimate just how much an IRA (Roth or regular) can do for them. That's because they don't understand what you do as an up-and-coming Automatic Millionaire—in order to make an IRA account really work for you in the real world, you need to **Make It Automatic**.

When I said before that it shouldn't take you more than an hour to set up an IRA, I included the time it would take to automate everything. I also included travel and waiting-in-line time. The actual paperwork to do everything needed to open an IRA and make it automatic can be completed in less than fifteen minutes. In fact, it's really not any more complicated than opening a checking account.

WHERE TO GO TO OPEN
AN IRA ACCOUNT

There are literally hundreds of banks, brokerage firms, and mutual fund companies you can choose from to help you open a Roth or traditional IRA account. Below are six firms I think make the process really easy. They are all large companies that offer online services with phone support, and all can help you automate the process in minutes. Though this is not an exhaustive list, it may be all you need to make a decision.

IF YOU WANT TO DO THIS FROM THE
COMFORT OF HOME . . .

TD Waterhouse
1-800-934-4448
www.tdwaterhouse.com

TD Waterhouse is consistently rated as one of the top firms for "do it yourself" investors. What's nice about these guys is that they have a really robust Internet site that can help you learn more about investing. I particularly like their retirement planning section, which helps you analyze which type of retirement account to use. They also make opening an account online incredibly easy. (While you are online, you can call them and speak with a live person who will walk you through the process.) Equally attractive, there's no minimum deposit requirement if you want to open a retirement account! What's more, you can set up an automatic investment program for mutual funds on as little as $100 a month. This is a huge advantage if you want to get started today but have little savings. In general, TD Waterhouse makes it easy to become an Automatic Millionaire, helping to arrange both payroll deduction plans with employers and money transfer programs, with banks, by which funds are automatically moved into your investment or retirement accounts. And for those who like to do business face-to-face, TD Waterhouse has more than 150 branch locations around the country.

ING Direct
1-800-ING-DIRECT
www.ingdirect.com

Owned by one of the largest financial service companies in the world, ING Direct is growing aggressively in the United States. Their aim is to make investing easy for small investors. Go to their web site and the first thing you'll notice is how incredibly simple it is to understand and use. ING Direct currently offers both traditional IRA and Roth IRA accounts, as well as a choice of nine mutual funds to invest in. All you need to do is select the one that matches your risk tolerance. What's more, there's no minimum investment requirement if you set up an automatic investment plan and commit to save $250 over the course of the year. ING also provides three asset allocation models on their web site using their six funds. You need to invest a minimum of $25 per month per fund to use their suggested models. The forms can be printed right off the web site, and company representatives will get on the phone with you if you need help filling them out. The closest thing to a catch here is that you have to have an ING Direct savings account in order to be able to open an IRA. (Fortunately, there's no minimum deposit requirement to open a savings account.)

ShareBuilder
1-866-747-2537
www.sharebuilder.com

ShareBuilder is on a mission to help investors get started investing automatically with small amounts of money. They have no minimum requirement to open an account, so it's easy to get started. Their IRA accounts allow you to set a monthly dollar amount, automatically debit the money from your checking account, and have the investments made for you year after year. They also have one of the lowest cost-pricing structures I've seen in the brokerage industry, plus a user-friendly web site and live phone and e-mail support to answer questions. You can start investing with as little as $50 a month and they're one of the few online brokerages that don't have hidden inactivity or maintenance fees.

If you want to open an account with them but aren't sure what to invest in, you can use their portfolio diversification tool called PlanBuilder. This free tool will help you select a mixture of exchange-traded index funds (ETFs), such as the S&P 500 Index, or choose individual stocks based on your personal investing profile. Similar to the way a 401(k) plan works, ShareBuilder automatically buys the stocks or ETFs that you designate every month, in the dollar amount you specify, without your having to worry about it. Everything is done online, completely automatically, as simple as can be.

Fidelity
1-800-Fidelity
www.fidelity.com

Fidelity is one of the leaders in making retirement simple. They have a great web site that is easy to use and understand. When you visit the site, go to the retirement area and look at the Fidelity Freedom Funds. These funds make investing simple by doing the asset allocation automatically for you based on your retirement date. The minimum investment required to open an IRA account and invest in a mutual fund is $2,500. However, if you set up an "automatic savings account," they will reduce that minimum requirement, provided you invest $250 per month.

Ameritrade
1-800-669-3900
www.ameritrade.com

Ameritrade, another major online brokerage firm that makes the process of opening your retirement account online easy, offers both Roth and deductible IRAs. They also make it easy for a small investor with a process they call Express Application. You can go to their web site and set all of this up automatically. You will need to start with an initial deposit of $500, but after that your monthly contributions can be as small as just one dollar. So you don't need to be rich to start and you don't need a lot of money to be able to invest automatically each month. They also offer over 11,000 mutual funds to choose from. Equally important, you can call someone on the phone and get help if you have questions while you're going through the set-up process online.

Vanguard
1-877-662-7447
www.vanguard.com

No list of investor-friendly brokerages would be complete without mentioning Vanguard, particularly if you plan to do it yourself long-term. Not only can they do everything the firms listed above do, but they also offer some of the lowest cost mutual funds in the industry. However, with Vanguard, you will need $1,000 to start a retirement account. But once you've started, you can contribute as little as $50 a month. Vanguard has an online tool that can help you open your retirement account in less then ten minutes. Their web site also offers great tools for retirement planning and how to select mutual funds. In particular, I like their free risk-tolerance test (you can find this under "Research Funds: Investor Questionnaire"). Again, with Vanguard you can call them on the phone (ask to speak with a retirement planning specialist) for help getting through the process online.

GOING TO A BROKERAGE
FIRM OR BANK

After looking at the company web sites I just described, you may decide that rather than going online, you'd prefer to walk into an actual office and set up your retirement account with a real person. There's nothing wrong with asking for help, and many people prefer to work face-to-face with a person they can get to know. If this describes you, the next few pages can be your guide.

COMPANIES THAT CAN HELP YOU

Telephone or go online to find the office nearest you.

FULL-SERVICE BROKERAGE FIRMS

AG Edwards
1-877-835-7877
www.agedwards.com

American Express
1-800-297-7378
www.americanexpress.com

Charles Schwab
1-866-855-9102
www.schwab.com

Edward Jones
1-314-515-2000
www.edwardjones.com

Fidelity Investments
1-800-FIDELITY
www.fidelity.com

Merrill Lynch
1-800-MERRILL
www.ml.com

Morgan Stanley
1-212-761-4000
www.morganstanley.com

Salomon Smith Barney
1-212-428-5200
www.smithbarney.com

NATIONAL BANKS

Bank of America
1-800-242-2632
www.bankofamerica.com

Citibank
1-800-248-4472
www.citibank.com

Washington Mutual
1-800-788-7000
www.wamu.com

Wells Fargo
1-800-869-3557
www.wellsfargo.com

MY GIFT TO YOU—

HIRING A FINANCIAL ADVISOR

One of the most commonly asked questions I've gotten from readers over the years is "How do I find a financial advisor?" To answer it, I've created an audio called "The 10 Golden Rules to Hiring a Financial Advisor." It's available as a free gift on my web site. To access it, simply visit **www.finishrich/advisor.** You may also want to take a look at my *Finish Rich Workbook*, which devotes an entire chapter to how to hire a financial advisor, including what questions to ask, where to research his or her background, what to watch out for, and how to pay for the service. It also contains a special tool called the Finish Rich Advisor Questionnaire and Gradecard™, which can be downloaded for free at the web site.

WHAT TO SAY WHEN YOU VISIT A BANK OR BROKERAGE FIRM

When you go into a bank or brokerage to open your IRA, make a point of telling the banker or broker assisting you (or the telephone representative, if you're opening your account online) that you want to set up a *systematic investment plan*. This is a plan under which money is automatically transferred on a regular basis into your IRA from some other account of yours (usually your regular checking account).

SETTING UP AN AUTOMATIC INVESTMENT PLAN

OPTION ONE: PAYROLL DEDUCTION

The best way to set up this sort of plan is to get your employer to do what is known as a payroll deduction, in which money is automatically taken out of your paycheck and transferred directly to your IRA. Not all employers are set up to do this. If yours is, they will give you a form to fill out that asks you to provide the account information they will need to be able to make the transfer (meaning you will need to open an IRA account and provide your employer with the account number and routing information). Some banks and brokerage firms will handle all this for you, contacting your employer's payroll department on your behalf and dealing with all the paperwork.

OPTION TWO: DEDUCTING FROM YOUR CHECKING ACCOUNT

If your employer doesn't offer payroll deduction, ask them if they provide automatic direct deposit (the answer will almost always be yes). This means they will directly deposit your paycheck into your checking account. If so, you can work with the bank or brokerage you hire to have the money automatically moved from your checking account to your retirement account . . . I suggest you arrange to have this done every time you're paid—ideally, the day after your paycheck clears.

Virtually every bank or brokerage that offers IRAs is equipped to make these arrangements for you. Many will even call your employer for you and help you complete the paperwork for automatic payroll deduction. All you've got to do is ask. And once it's done, you don't have to think about it anymore. What's more, your decision is not set in stone. You can usually change the arrangement with a simple phone call or written request. And don't forget that many banks now offer free online bill payment, which allows you to "autopay" a check to whomever you designate. This can make automating your investment plan a one-time, five-minute job.

ANOTHER INCREDIBLY SIMPLE WAY TO AUTOMATE EVERYTHING

Today's Internet technology makes it unbelievably simple to set up what is called "online bill pay." As the name suggests, online bill pay allows you to pay all of your bills online. Once you open an online bill pay account, your bills go directly to the company providing the service, which scans them and then presents them to you online. All you have to do to pay them is click a button. The funds to cover each bill are automatically taken out of your bank account. What's nice about online bill payment is that you can use it to send money to wherever you like automatically. Say you want to fund your retirement account with $50 a week. Online bill pay can do this for you every week without your "doing anything" other than setting it up. The cost to open an online bill payment service should run you about $12.95 a month (usually for thirty bills or checks) or $4.95 a month plus 50 cents for each bill. I've used this type of service for years for both my personal and business bills, and I think it's great.

Three established online bill pay companies are:

www.paytrust.com
www.statusfactory.com
www.quickenbillpay.com

Today, you can also use "Online Bill Pay" at most banks or brokerage firms. In many cases this online automated bill pay system can direct where you want your checks sent automatically at no cost.

HOW MUCH SHOULD I SAVE?

Compared with a 401(k) or a 403(b) plan, it doesn't take much to max out an IRA. As of 2006, the most you can contribute if you are under fifty is $4,000 a year. (If you're over fifty, the maximum is $5,000.) This works out to just $333 a month, or about $16 a working day. Unless you make less than $16 an hour, there's no reason you shouldn't max out your contributions. Remember, you are now supposed to be working at least one hour a day for yourself.

TRADITIONAL AND ROTH IRA CONTRIBUTION LIMITS		
Year	Maximum Allowable (if age 49 or younger)	Maximum Allowable (if age 50 or older)
2002	$3,000	$3,500
2003	$3,000	$3,500
2004	$3,000	$3,500
2005	$4,000	$4,500
2006	$4,000	$5,000
2007	$4,000	$5,000
2008	$5,000	$6,000

Note: After 2008, increases will be adjusted for inflation in $500 increments.

BUT CAN I REALLY GET RICH SAVING JUST $4,000 A YEAR?

Putting aside $4,000 a year may not sound like much, but don't forget the power of compound interest. If at age twenty-five you started putting $333 a month (or $4,000 a year) into an IRA that earned an annual return of 10 percent, by the time you were sixty-five, you'd have a nest egg worth nearly $2 million. Even if you waited until you were forty to get started, you'd still wind up with a hefty sum—roughly $434,000.

Obviously, the earlier you start, the easier it is to accumulate major wealth. Still, it's never too late to begin. The time to start is now. Some money is better than no money. (Go back and take another look at the chart on page 97.)

IT'S EVEN BETTER IF
YOU'RE SELF-EMPLOYED

If you are self-employed, I've got one thing to say to you: Congratulations. Small business truly powers our economy; it's the engine that creates economic growth. Recognizing this, the government gives business owners the best tax breaks when it comes to retirement accounts.

There are numerous types of retirement accounts business owners can select. Because this book is designed to get you to take action quickly, I'm going to discuss only two of them— the SEP IRA, which I regard as the most straightforward and uncomplicated retirement account there is for self-employed people, and the brand-new One-Person 401(k) Profit Sharing Account, which is really exciting.[1]

THE JOYS OF SEP IRAs

The SEP in SEP IRA stands for Simplified Employee Pension, otherwise known as a self-employed retirement account. As a result of the tax law changes in 2002, these plans are truly amazing. You can now contribute as much as 25 percent of

---

[1] If you're interested in other retirement accounts for business owners such as 401(k)/Profit Sharing Accounts, Money Purchase Plans, Profit Sharing Plans, Defined Benefits Plans, and SIMPLE plans, you can read all about them in detail in any of my three previous books— *Smart Women Finish Rich*, *Smart Couples Finish Rich*, and *The Finish Rich Workbook*. You can also visit my web site at www.finishrich.com to read a free chapter on this topic.

your gross income to a SEP IRA up to a maximum of more than $42,000 (the amount is adjusted for inflation every year). How's that for Paying Yourself First?

If you are self-employed and don't have any employees, run—don't walk—to the nearest bank or brokerage and open a SEP IRA today (use the lists on pages 102–7). Almost all of the firms listed there offer SEP IRAs. The only slightly complicated part of the process is setting it up to work automatically. That's because as a self-employed person, you probably don't draw a regular salary. Still, as with the other retirement plans we've discussed, the key to making this work is automation, so it's worth taking the trouble to figure it out.

Here is what you do:

If you draw a regular salary: Set up your payroll system to automatically transfer contributions to your SEP IRA. This should be especially easy if you use a payroll company. As with the other plans, the idea should be to Pay Yourself First roughly 10 percent of your income—more if you want to be really rich. (Remember, the SEP IRA rules permit you to go as high as 25 percent.)

If you don't draw a regular salary: Many self-employed people wait until most of their business expenses have been paid before they draw any salary or bonuses for themselves. If this is what you do, then you simply must make sure that every time you take money out of your business, you funnel the first 10 percent to your SEP IRA. As this may be difficult if not impossible to automate, I would recommend that you try to pay yourself some sort of salary simply so you won't have to think about funding your plan. As I hope you've learned by now, processes that are automated are the ones that work. Processes that aren't usually don't.

THE BRAND-NEW ONE-PERSON 401(K)/PROFIT-SHARING PLAN

This new plan is truly amazing. As a result of the 2002 tax law changes, you can now open up a 401(k) plan for a one-person business at a cost of as little as $150. You can then fund it with up to 100 percent of the first $14,000 you earn in 2005 (more in later years). On top of that, you can use the profit-sharing portion of the plan to contribute up to another 25 percent of your income. The combined total you could contribute in 2005 was $42,000. (This figure will be ratcheted up to account for inflation over the coming years.)

Check out this math. Say you earned $50,000 as a self-employed businessperson. With a One-Person 401(k)/Profit-Sharing Plan, you could put the first $12,000 you earned into the 401(k) account and then put another $12,500 into the profit-sharing portion. That's a total of $24,500 in pretax savings—on a $50,000 income! This is why business owners can get rich faster than regular workers. If you use a payroll company like Paychex or ADP, ask them for details because they are now making these plans available. In addition, most full-service financial firms, including mutual fund companies, should be offering them soon (if they aren't already), so be sure to check with them as well (see page 107 for how to reach them).

Among the companies you can contact for details on these

exciting new plans are Aim Funds (www.aimfunds.com), John Hancock Funds (www.jhancock.com), and Pioneer Funds (www.pioneerfunds.com). In most cases, it will cost you as little as $150 to open one of these plans. My wife, Michelle, and I set up one of these plans for our business in 2002 and it took all of twenty minutes to sign up and automate everything.

SO HOW SHOULD I INVEST MY RETIREMENT MONEY?

Now that we've looked at the different types of retirement accounts that are available, let's look at what to do with the money you put in your plan. Whether you open a 401(k) plan at work or an IRA or SEP IRA on your own, once your money is deposited in the account you need to select an investment. The account itself is just a holding tank. It's the investment you select that determines how fast your money will grow. Whether it earns 1 percent or 10 percent depends on how you invest it. With a retirement account, it's critical that you invest wisely, not gamble.

The best way to do this is to follow the old advice about not putting all your eggs in one basket. In other words, you've got to diversify—which means that instead of investing all of your money in just one or two places, you spread it around. Now spreading your money around does not mean opening up a lot of different retirement accounts in different places. If you do that and then make the same kinds of investments with each of them, all you've done is complicate your life. Spreading your money around means building a diversified portfolio of stocks, bonds, and cash investments all done in *one* retirement account. Many people make this complicated. It doesn't need to be.

THE POWER OF THE PYRAMID

On page 119 is a wonderful tool designed to help you determine where your money should be invested and how much should go in each place. I call it the Automatic Millionaire Investment Pyramid, and it's based on two simple principles: (1) that your money should be invested in a combination of cash, bonds, and stocks; and (2) that the nature of this combination should change over time as your life situation changes.

As you can see, the pyramid divides your financial life into four distinct periods: the "getting started" years, the "making money" years, the "preretirement" years, and the "retirement" years. At each point, your needs and goals are different, and as a result you should probably have a different combination of investments.

Within each period, the pyramid suggests what percentage of your nest egg should be allocated to each of five standard types of investments. In order of risk, from safest to most risky, these are cash, bonds, income investments, growth investments, growth & income investments, and aggressive growth investments.

The base of the pyramid rests on the safest investments (cash and bonds). As you work your way up the pyramid, you take on more risk, moving from growth & income to growth to aggressive growth. Aside from the fact that you always want your retirement account to be built from the ground up with safe investments first, the mixture of risk categories that's right for you depends on your age. The younger you are, the more risk you can afford, since you have more time to ride out a bad stock market or other economic downturn. The opposite is true for someone who's already retired. The principle is amazingly simple, and what's more, it actually works.

Use the investment pyramid as a guide to select what kind of investments to make with the money in your retirement accounts. Rather than looking for individual stocks and bonds that match the particular risk profile that is right for your situation, I suggest you put your money in appropriate mutual funds. Mutual funds not only offer professional money management, diversification, and ease of use, but most now allow you to start investing with as little as $50. Some even accept monthly investments as low as $25. Over the next few pages, I'll share my favorite type of funds for investors who are just starting out.

THE AUTOMATIC MILLIONAIRE INVESTMENT PYRAMID

TEENS TO THIRTIES (The "Getting Started" Years)

Situation and goals
- Aggressive
- Growing net worth
- Very long-term outlook
- Willing to take a fair amount of risk

5% to 10% Aggressive Growth

40% to 50% Growth

30% to 40% Growth & Income

5% to 15% Bonds

5% to 10% Cash

THIRTIES TO FIFTIES (The "Making Money" Years)

Situation and goals
- Ten or more years to retirement
- Building net worth
- Willing to take risk
- Not needing investment income

5% to 10% Aggressive Growth

25% to 35% Growth

35% to 45% Growth & Income

15% to 25% Bonds

5% to 10% Cash

FIFTY TO MID-SIXTIES (The "Preretirement" Years)

Situation and goals
- Less than ten years to retirement
- Typically high-income years with fewer financial responsibilities
- Willing to take some risk but wanting less volatility

0 to 5% Aggressive Growth

15% to 25% Growth

30% to 40% Growth & Income

20% to 30% Bonds

5% to 10% Cash

SIXTIES AND UP (The "Retirement" Years)

Situation and goals
- Enjoying retirement or very close to retiring
- Protecting net worth
- Preferring less risk

0 to 5% Aggressive Growth

10% to 20% Growth

30% to 40% Growth & Income

25% to 35% Bonds

10% to 15% Cash

WHAT ABOUT INVESTING
IN MY 401(k) PLAN?

The investment pyramid can help you select how to allocate the money you put into your 401(k) plan. Chances are, your plan will offer you a menu of investment choices quite similar (if not identical) to the ones listed in the pyramid. If so, you can simply use the percentages from the pyramid to distribute your dollars appropriately. The only noticeable difference may be that if you happen to work for a large, publicly traded company, your plan will also offer you the chance to invest in your company's stock. If it does, please resist the temptation to overinvest—no matter how great you think your company is.

In recent years, too many overly loyal employees have lost their entire nest eggs because they invested all their retirement money in their own company's stock. Keep in mind names like Enron, WorldCom, and Lucent Technologies. Until the roof fell in, everyone thought these companies were sure things—no one more than the people who worked for them. In my view, you should never invest more than 25 percent—and if you want to be conservative, not more than 5 percent—of your retirement money in your own company's stock. Moreover, when you use the Automatic Millionaire Investment Pyramid, consider your company's stock to be an aggressive growth investment (even if it's a conservative company). This is because owning a single stock reduces your diversification—and therefore increases your risk.

SUPERSIMPLE ONE-STOP SHOPPING

Many company retirement plans offer participants a one-stop mutual fund choice that combines under one "roof" all the different kinds of investments you need to make. As a result, you don't need to worry about whether you may have confused an aggressive growth fund with just a growth fund, and vice versa. Nor do you need to figure out what percentage of your money should go into bonds versus stocks.

This supersimple kind of investment goes by a variety of names. Depending on the plan, it might be called an asset allocation fund or a fund of funds or a life stage fund. Some of these funds have a specific year in their name (for example, the 2020 fund or the 2030 fund), the idea being that you select the fund closest to your projected retirement date. Most companies also offer what is called a balanced fund. A balanced fund offers professional management and an asset allocation that is typically 60 percent stock and 40 percent bonds.

WHY BALANCED FUNDS AND ASSET
ALLOCATION FUNDS MAKE SENSE

An asset allocation or balanced fund does all the work for you, offering the right mix of cash, bonds, and stocks in one fund. You don't have to create an Automatic Millionaire Investment Pyramid. As a result, these kinds of funds make the process of investing really easy. I can't emphasize that enough. And you don't have to work for a company with a 401(k) plan to make use of them. You can invest in preselected and professionally managed asset allocation funds through a traditional IRA, Roth IRA, or SEP IRA.

If you are working with a financial advisor at a bank or brokerage firm, tell him or her that you'd like to look at **asset allocation fund** and **balanced fund** options. Your advisor should be able to point you in the right direction. In addition, I've highlighted some full-service options below. If you want to do this yourself, there are ways to invest without a broker or advisor. To get you started, here is a list (in no particular order) of companies that offer asset allocation and balanced funds.

ASSET ALLOCATION FUNDS
AND BALANCED FUNDS

THE "DO IT YOURSELF" OPTION

The following companies offer funds for "do it yourself" investing, meaning you don't need a financial advisor to purchase the funds. What's more, most of these funds are no-load funds—meaning you can invest in them without having to pay a commission.

Vanguard
1-877-662-7447
www.vanguard.com

Ask about the Vanguard Life Strategy Funds (Vanguard's asset allocation funds). Also ask about the Vanguard STAR

Fund (this is a "fund of funds" asset allocation product created using various Vanguard funds). Finally, ask about the Vanguard Balanced Fund, a very low-cost balanced fund with an excellent long-term track record.

Fidelity Investments
1-800-FIDELITY
www.fidelity.com

Ask about the Fidelity Freedom Funds. These asset allocation funds come with a due date (e.g., 2000, 2010, 2020, 2030, 2040). The idea is that you invest in the fund with the date closest to when you think you're going to want to start taking money out of the fund (e.g., when you plan to retire). Also ask about the Fidelity Balanced Fund.

Charles Schwab
1-866-855-9102
www.schwab.com

Ask about the Schwab Market Track series of funds. Schwab currently offers four funds in this series, ranging from conservative to growth. Also ask about Schwab's Balanced MarketMasters funds.

T. Rowe Price
1-877-804-2315
www.troweprice.com

Ask about the T. Rowe Price Retirement series. Like the Fidelity Freedom Funds, these funds come with a due date. Also ask about the T. Rowe Price Spectrum Funds.

American Century
1-800-345-2021
www.americancentury.com

Ask about the American Century Strategic Asset Allocation Funds. There are three of them: conservative, moderate,
and aggressive.

Scudder
1-800-621-1048
www.scudder.com

Ask about the Scudder Pathway Funds. Scudder offers
three: moderate, conservative, and growth.

THE FULL-SERVICE OPTION

When you use a full-service financial advisor or banker, all
you need to do is tell him or her that you are interested in
looking at an asset allocation fund or a balanced fund. Almost
every company listed on page 107 will offer you a variety to
select from. The following companies offer a proprietary fund
product (meaning they created the fund and/or manage it).
Even if balanced funds and asset allocation appeal to you
because they are super simple and one-stop, you may still
prefer doing business face to face with a banker or a financial
advisor rather than doing it yourself.

Wells Fargo
1-800-222-8222
www.wellsfargo.com

Wells Fargo offers both Asset Allocation Funds (with due dates) and strategically managed Asset Allocation Funds (called "Wealth Builder Funds"). Ask about both.

Washington Mutual
1-800-222-5852
www.wamu.com

Ask about the WM Strategic Asset Management funds. They refer to them as "SAM" portfolios. They currently offer five "fund of fund" products. For details on these funds, visit www.wmgroupoffunds.com

Bank of America
1-800-321-7854
www.bankofamerica.com

Ask about the Nations LifeGoal funds. They include three asset allocation funds (income & growth, balanced growth, growth).

Bank One
1-877-226-5663
www.bankone.com

Ask about the funds called One Group Investor. There are three asset allocation funds (conservative growth, growth & income, and investors growth).

Putnam Funds
1-800-225-1581
www.putnamfunds.com

Putnam funds are sold through full-service financial advisors such as Morgan Stanley, Merrill Lynch, and Edward Jones. Ask your advisor to show you the three Putnam Asset Allocation Funds: conservative, balanced, and growth.

Van Kampen Investments
1-800-341-2911
www.vankampen.com

Van Kampen funds are also sold through full-service financial advisors. Ask them about the Van Kampen Equity and Income fund. It's been around since 1960 and has a solid long-term track record with a balanced approach to investing.

INVESTING MADE SIMPLE

Does investing all of your retirement money in a single fund seem too easy, too good to be true? Even a bit boring? Over the years, as a financial advisor, an investor, and a money coach, I've seen really great markets, so-so markets, and absolutely horrific markets (like the one we just lived through from 2000 through the first quarter of 2003). If I've learned one true secret to being an investor who does well in both good times and bad, it is this: MANAGING YOUR MONEY SHOULD BE BORING!

If you invest your money according to the Automatic Millionaire Investment Pyramid, as I suggest on page 119, you will end up with a well-diversified portfolio that is professionally managed. Even better, if you invest in one balanced fund or asset allocation fund that diversifies your portfolio for you AND you automate your contributions—which, after all, is the point of this little book—you'll have a really boring financial life. Your money will be totally diversified, professionally balanced and managed, and your savings plan will be on automatic pilot.

Of course, if you did this, you'd have nothing to talk about at cocktail parties when people bring up the subject of how they are investing their money. No one brags about having a really simple, well-diversified investment portfolio. So you'd need to find something else to talk about at parties. But, really, wouldn't you like that to be your biggest problem?

HOW TO PROTECT YOUR FORTUNE IN A BAD MARKET

Whether you diversify your investments using the Automatic Millionaire Investment Pyramid or by using a balanced fund or an asset allocation fund, the bottom-line reason why you should is that diversification can protect your life's savings in a bad market. The chart on page 128 shows how diversification saved the day even in the horrible market that we all just lived through between 2000 and 2002. It shows how a portfolio diversified among stocks, bonds, and Treasury bills nearly maintained its value while the same amount of money invested in stocks alone lost nearly half its value. If fear of losing everything in a stock market crash has held you back from starting a retirement plan, this chart should reassure you that diversification is your protection.

VALUE OF A $10,000 INVESTMENT IN 2000–2002 BEAR MARKET

Source: Ibbotson Associates. Diversified Portfolio: 25% S&P 500 Index; 25% Ibbotson Small Co. Stocks; 25% Treasury Bills; 25% Lehman Brothers Government/Corporate Bonds Index. Non-diversified Portfolio: S&P 500 Index.

LEARNING MORE ABOUT YOUR INVESTMENT CHOICES

The Internet is a great resource as you make decisions about how to invest in your 401(k) or other retirement plans. Here are some sites to check out. I've highlighted some of my favorite features that can help you choose funds.

SOME GREAT WEB SITES FOR
RESEARCHING MUTUAL FUNDS, STOCKS,
AND GENERAL FINANCIAL PLANNING

WWW.MORNINGSTAR.COM

This is the place to start. Morningstar is the company that really originated the concept of ranking mutual funds. It also created the star system to score them. Go to the Morningstar home page and click on "Mutual Funds." Then click on a section called "Fund Quickrank." For fun, start by screening "U.S. Stock Funds" by "Total return %: 10 Year Annualized." Just three clicks and—bam! You've got a list of the top performing U.S. funds over the last ten years. Another impressive feature of the Morningstar site is its fund reports, which provide a general description of virtually every fund there is along with an in-depth analysis that is easy to read and understand. You can also research individual stocks. You have to subscribe to Morningstar to get their detailed assessments, but general summaries are available for free.

HTTP://FINANCE.YAHOO.COM

Yahoo offers a true full-service financial portal, with stock and mutual fund analysis, portfolio tracking, online bill paying, message boards, research, and, much, much more. Yahoo makes it easy for you to get the information you need quickly and for free. Try the following as a kind of test drive. Visit this site and click on "Mutual Funds." Then click on the mutual fund screener. When it asks you for qualifications, select "Any U.S. Stock Funds," at longer than 5 years of tenure, with a minimum initial investment of less than $10,000, and rank by performance. Bam! In literally seconds, you'll have a long list of funds that have generated an average return of better than 10 percent a year. From there, you can screen for a fund that meets your particular requirements (such as one that requires an initial investment of less than $1,000). This is just one example of what this site can do. There is a wealth of free information here to help you.

WWW.MFEA.COM

Looking for a quick list of mutual funds that let you invest less than $50 a month? Visit this web site's fund center, where you'll find a long list of mutual funds companies that welcome small investors. You'll also find valuable educational information on the benefits of mutual fund investing and tons of free tools to help you learn more.

WWW.SMARTMONEY.COM

Created by the editors of *Smart Money* magazine, this is a terrific site, easy to use and fun to work with. There are so many articles on this site that you could spend hours here and just scratch the surface. My favorite part of this site is the Personal Financial Planning section. There's also a great section in this area on retirement planning and tons of tools.

WWW.NYSE.COM

The official site of the New York Stock Exchange, NYSE.com contains detailed data about every NYSE-listed company as well as solid background information on how the exchange works.

WWW.NASDAQ.COM

For real-time stock quotes and detailed information about any of the more than 4,000 companies listed on the NASDAQ stock market, this is the place to go.

THE AUTOMATIC MILLIONAIRE COLUMN ON YAHOO! FINANCE

For additional resources, motivational stories, and financial tips read my bi-weekly column *The Automatic Millionaire* on Yahoo! Finance. Visit http://finance.yahoo.com or my web site www.finishrich.com to read the archives.

DO YOU HAVE MORE QUESTIONS ABOUT RETIREMENT ACCOUNTS?

Any questions you may still have about retirement accounts are bound to be covered in one of two enormously useful pamphlets you can get for free from the Internal Revenue Service. Go online to www.irs.gov and request Publication #590 *(Individual Retirement Arrangements)* and Publication #560 *(Retirement Plans for Small Businesses)*. You can download these booklets right off the Internet.

If you haven't visited the IRS's new web site, check it out. It contains an amazing amount of information that can help you, and it's all free. Believe it or not, the government really wants you to save money by making pretax contributions to a qualified retirement plan. You just need to know how to do it. If you don't have access to the Internet, you can call the IRS toll-free at 1-800-829-3676 and request the reports. Also, the IRS now maintains toll-free hotlines you can call to get assistance. For tax questions, call 1-800-829-1040. For additional information on free IRS services, request Publication #910 (*Guide to Free Tax Services*).

WHATEVER YOU DO, REMEMBER TO MAKE IT AUTOMATIC

The McIntyres didn't become millionaires by being disciplined and sitting down once every two weeks to write a check to their retirement accounts. They were just as busy and distracted as you are. If they had had to write a check every few weeks, they would still be living paycheck to paycheck. What enabled them to achieve millionaire status was the action they took to make saving for the future AUTOMATIC. So if your current plan is not automatic, you need to change it.

By the same token, if you're not funneling at least 10 percent of your income into a tax-deferred retirement account, you need to change that too. Don't settle for saving 4 percent of your income like most people. Most people end up at retirement dependent on Social Security, friends, and family for survival. You've got the knowledge now to do better. So do better. Even if you feel you have to do it gradually, do it.

Retirement planning can be as simple or as challenging as you decide to make it. With what you've learned so far, you can make it really simple—and amazingly effective.

AUTOMATIC MILLIONAIRE ACTION STEPS

Here's what you should be doing right now to ensure yourself a worry-free retirement.

❏ Make sure you're signed up for your retirement account at work.

❏ If you don't have a retirement plan at work, open an IRA.

❏ If you are self-employed, open a SEP IRA or a One-Person 401(k)/Profit-Sharing Plan.

❏ Decide how much you are going to contribute to your account each month (ideally, the maximum amount allowed).

❏ Decide how you want to invest your retirement contributions.

❏ Whatever type of account you open, arrange to have your contributions AUTOMATICALLY transferred into it, either through payroll deduction at work or an automatic investment plan run by the bank or brokerage firm where you've set up your retirement account.

Now let's go learn how to buy yourself financial security in case of a rainy day.

CHAPTER FIVE

AUTOMATE FOR A RAINY DAY

THE "SLEEP WELL AT NIGHT" FACTOR

If the only actions you take as a result of reading this book are to decide to Pay Yourself First for your future and Make It Automatic, you'd still be better off than the vast majority of people. After all, how many friends or acquaintances do you have who can look forward to the future knowing they won't have any money worries in their later years?

But what about now? How can you provide yourself with some financial security today?

This chapter answers two basic questions: How much

money should you put aside in order to protect yourself against the proverbial "rainy day," and where should you put it?

Let's face it. No matter how well you plan or how positively you think, there are always things out of your control that can go wrong—sometimes really wrong. People lose their jobs, their health, their spouses. The economy can go sour, the stock market can drop, businesses can go bankrupt. Circumstances change. If there's anything you can count on, it's that life is filled with unexpected changes. Stuff happens.

Some people worry about change, while others prepare for it. As an Automatic Millionaire, you prepare. That way, when you hit a bump in the road, you don't have to borrow against your future—or raid your Pay Yourself First money—to deal with the problem.

Here's a simple test you can take right now to determine if you are prepared for the kind of changes the real world can (and will) throw at you.

THE "SLEEP WELL AT NIGHT" TEST

My monthly expenses currently total: $_____

I currently have $_____ saved in a money market or checking account.

This equals _____ [insert number] months' worth of expenses.

Stop reading. Go and grab a pen or pencil and fill in the blanks above to find out where you stand.

You don't need to pull out your checkbook to figure this out. Just estimate what you think you spend each month, what you know you have in the bank, and how many months' worth of expenses your current balance can cover.

A GOOD NIGHT'S SLEEP OR THE WORRY OF BANKRUPTCY?

So how did you do? How many months' worth of savings do you currently have?

Earlier, I mentioned that according to the latest statistics, the average American has less than three months' worth of expenses set aside. In my personal experience as a financial advisor, I've found that most people don't even have that much. Chances are that your neighbor, the one driving the new leased car and drinking two lattes a day, has less than one month's worth of expenses set aside.

Personal bankruptcies have been on the rise in the United States, with more than 1.6 million in 2004. And in future years, it will likely get worse. My prediction is that it won't be long before foreclosures on personal residences will also be reaching record levels.

Why? The answer is simple: We simply don't maintain the same cushion of emergency money that our parents and grandparents routinely stashed away. Instead, we are literally living paycheck to paycheck. In most families, it's actually two paychecks to two paychecks. (Nearly three out of every four American homes are two-income households.) If one of those paychecks disappears, the family that depends on it can find itself upside-down financially in less than six months.

YOUR GOAL:
BUILD AN EMERGENCY
BASKET OF CASH

To make sure this never happens to you, I'm going to show you how to build an emergency basket of cash AUTOMATI-CALLY.

Grandma Bach used to tell me, "David, when the going gets tough, the tough have cash." In this, as in so many other things, she knew what she was talking about. Cash is king. Cash is security. Cash is protection. Cash is your "take this job and shove it" option.

Cash is just like the seat belt you buckle when you get behind the wheel of your car. When you go for a drive, you don't plan to have an accident. Still, you wear your seat belt because (1) someone else could run into you, and (2) stuff happens.

It's the same with money. You may never plan on losing your job or becoming disabled or having your house burn down, but like I said, stuff happens. It always has and it always will. Fortunately, that doesn't mean you have to be worried all the time. There is a way to protect yourself financially from the uncertainties of life. How? By surrounding yourself with a cushion of money.

THE THREE RULES OF
EMERGENCY MONEY

1. Decide how big a cushion you need.

In order to be a real Automatic Millionaire, I believe you need a cash cushion of at least three months' worth of expenses. Take what you estimate you spend each month, multiply it by three, and you've calculated your goal for emergency savings.

If you typically spend $3,000 a month, you want to have at least $9,000 put away in a reserve account not to be touched unless there's an emergency. Should you try to save more? Absolutely. In my previous books, I've suggested putting aside anywhere from three to twenty-four months' worth of expenses, depending on your situation. How much you should save depends on what you feel you need to "sleep well at night." Three months' worth is a great starting place, but if you want to go higher, by all means do what feels right to you.

With all the economic and political unrest in the world these days, a year's worth of expenses is a great ultimate goal to shoot for. With that much saved, you don't have to worry about making ends meet even if you lose your job and can't find a new one for a while. Even more important, a one-year cushion gives you the freedom to make decisions about your life that you might not feel able to make now—like whether to leave a job you don't like so you can risk trying a new career.

2. Don't touch it.

The reason most people don't have any emergency money in the bank is that they have what they think is an emergency every month. I want you to imagine that your emergency money is like the fire extinguisher on the wall in an office building. The cabinet containing the fire extinguisher usually bears a sign that reads, "In case of emergency, break glass." It doesn't say, "If you think you smell smoke, break glass." Think of your emergency fund the same way.

The imaginary instruction sign on your emergency fund doesn't say, "In case you really need a new dress for that special party . . ." or "In case the latest golf club has just gone on sale at the sporting goods store . . ." or "In case you want a new dishwasher because the old one is making noise . . ." It says, "Don't touch me unless it's a real emergency."

What's a real emergency? Be honest with yourself. You know what a real emergency is. A real emergency is something that threatens your survival, not just your desire to be comfortable.

3. Put it in the right place.

I once conducted a seminar where I talked about how important it is to have some money set aside in case of emergency. In the middle of my discussion, a gentleman named Bob sitting in the back of the room raised his hand. "David," he said, "I've got $60,000 in emergency funds put away. Is that enough?"

"That depends," I replied. "How much do you spend each month?"

"About $2,000," came the answer.

"So you've got thirty months' worth of expenses put away," I said. "That's a HUGE emergency fund by any standard. Why so much?"

Bob grinned an embarrassed sort of grin. "Well," he said, "you know, my wife and I worry about the possibility of another depression, or maybe a war. My wife even worries about UFOs."

The class started laughing.

"No, no," I said, quieting them down. "Remember, the point of an emergency fund is so you can sleep well at night. If having sixty months' worth of expenses keeps Bob and his wife from worrying about UFOs, then that's the right amount of money for them to have saved." I turned back to Bob. "So tell me," I continued, "how much interest are you earning on this money?"

Bob's answer stopped me in my tracks. "I'm not earning any interest on the money," he said. "I've got it buried in my backyard in a suitcase."

I stared at him in disbelief. "You've got $60,000 in cash buried in a suitcase in your backyard?"

"Well, it's really more like $65,000," he said. "There's some gold coins in the suitcase too."

At this point, I was speechless. In the silence that followed, someone in the front row turned to Bob and said, "Out of curiosity, where exactly do you live?"

The class broke up completely. It was one of the funniest moments I've ever experienced in a classroom. People were laughing for minutes.

All the same, however, Bob's story troubled me. No way was he one of a kind. It's not that I thought there were lots of people burying their money in suitcases. But there had to be thousands, maybe even millions of people out there putting aside money for a rainy day without earning any interest on it. And that's almost as bad as what Bob did.

You heard me right. Not earning interest on your emergency money is almost as bad as burying it in your backyard.

MAKE THE MOST OF YOUR EMERGENCY FUNDS

When most people set up emergency funds, they put their "rainy day" money in savings and checking accounts. Why is this a bad deal? Because most savings and checking accounts pay little if any interest. In fact, most of these accounts can even cost you money—what with monthly fees, ATM fees, check fees, visiting the branch fees, and so on.

The point is that whatever you do with your emergency money, find a bank you can trust that will take care of your money but will also make it grow. What you want to do with your emergency money is put it in a money market account that pays reasonable interest.

A money market account is one of the simplest and most secure alternatives around for anyone who wants to put aside some cash and earn a reasonable return on it. When you make a deposit in a money market account, you are actually buying shares in a money market fund—a mutual fund that invests in the safest and most liquid securities there are: very short-term government bonds and sometimes highly rated corporate bonds. Just a few years ago, you generally needed a minimum of as much as $10,000 to open a money market account. Because of this, many people still mistakenly think these accounts are for the rich. In fact, you can now open most money market accounts with a minimum deposit of between $1,000 and $2,000—and in a few selected cases with as a little as one dollar. That's right—just one dollar.

SHOP FOR A RATE LIKE YOU'D SHOP FOR A CAR

These days, there are literally thousands of money market accounts to choose from, and like everything else, the cost and quality varies widely. So, just as if you were buying a car, don't be afraid to shop around.

Perhaps the most important variable is the interest rate different money market accounts pay. Not only is there a huge variation from bank to bank, but rates can and do change daily.

Since the early 1990s, interest rates in general have been dropping steadily—and along with them so have the rates paid by most money market accounts. Over that time, I've seen them go from about 12 percent a year to a solid 7 percent in the 1990s to 1 to 3 percent as of this writing (in early 2005).

FINDING THE RATE MONEY MARKET ACCOUNTS ARE PAYING

To get an up-to-date look at what rates are available, here is what you should do.

1. Get a copy of a financial publication such as the *Wall Street Journal, Investors Business Daily,* or *Barron's.* They all offer extensive lists of what interest rates different money market funds are paying. Similar information (though not quite so detailed) can also be found in *USA Today* or possibly even your local paper.

2. Go to www.bankrate.com if you have access to the Internet. This web site not only allows you to compare money market rates being offered by different institutions but also indicates the minimum deposit each requires to open an account. In addition, it allows you to sort banks by state, which is important since some banks can offer tax-free checking and money market accounts, depending on which state they—and you—happen to be in.

NOW CALL YOUR BANK

Once you've gotten an idea of what kind of rates are available, you'll be in a better position to question the institution that is currently holding your rainy day money. If it's a bank, pick up the phone and call them. Ask what kind of interest your money is earning. If the answer is zero, ask if they offer money market accounts. If they do, ask them what you need to do to open one and how much interest it would pay. Then compare the rates to what you've seen elsewhere.

Based on this comparison, you may decide that it makes sense simply to move your emergency funds from the non- or low-interest-bearing account they're in now to a money market fund at the same bank. If this turns out to be the case, keep in mind that all it took for your money to start earning interest was for you to start asking the right questions. Why didn't the bank tell you this information earlier? What do you think? This is why knowledge is power.

Remember, the rich get rich because they make their money work for them. Now it's your turn to do the same.

FOR AN EVEN BETTER DEAL, CHECK OUT BROKERAGE FIRMS

In most cases, you can get a higher yielding money market account at a brokerage firm than at your local bank. There are many reputable brokerages that offer money market accounts. The list on the next few pages is not exhaustive, but it's a great start—and more than likely contains enough leads for you to be able to make a decision.

When you contact a brokerage firm, ask the following questions:

1. What's the minimum to invest?
2. Can I set up a systematic investment program where

you take money out of my checking account on a regular basis and invest it in a money market account? (Make sure they can do this automatically.)

3. If I set up a systematic investment plan, will you lower the minimum to invest?

4. Do you offer federally insured accounts? What's the rate on your insured money market accounts vs. your regular money market accounts?

5. Does the account come with check-writing privileges, and if so, what's the smallest check you can write? Does it come with an ATM card? (Even though you're not going to use your checks or ATM card except in an emergency, it's nice to have them in case you ever need quick access to your funds.)

6. Does the bank charge a low balance fee? (Some accounts hit you with an extra monthly or annual fee if you dip below a minimum. Be sure to ask for details.)

PLACES TO OPEN A
MONEY MARKET ACCOUNT

I've listed the following banks and brokerages according to how small a minimum deposit they require to open a money market account, starting with the lowest minimum and ending with the highest. You should compare which company offers the best rates and lowest fees as new products are constantly being offered.

EmigrantDirect.com (No minimum required to invest)
1-800-836-1997
www.emigrantdirect.com

EmigrantDirect.com (a division of Emigrant Savings Bank, an FDIC insured bank, which has been in business since 1850) offers one of the highest-rate savings accounts available today. In fact, as of the writing of this edition, they offer an incredible 3.5 percent annual yield on their AmericanDream Savings Account™. These accounts do not require a minimum deposit to get started, so it may make sense to move your existing savings accounts if this rate is better. You can set up a new account in minutes on their web site, and easily link it directly to your regular checking account, all with no fees of any kind. And best of all, with these accounts you can place your savings program on autopilot with automatic recurring deposits over time.

ING Direct (No minimum required to invest)
1-800-ING-DIRECT
www.ingdirect.com

As I noted earlier, ING Direct is working hard to build its business in the United States. One of the ways in which they are doing this is by offering some of the highest money markets rates around, with *no minimum investment required*. What I particularly like about them is that you can set up an ING Direct account online and arrange for money to be transferred into it automatically from your checking account in just a few minutes without ever leaving home. If you have any questions, you can call them and they will walk you through the process on the phone. In addition to offering one of the highest interest rates around, ING Direct is one of the very few financial institutions whose money market accounts are FDIC insured. They call this account the Orange Savings Account, and except for the fact that it does not offer check-writing privileges, it's a pretty good deal.

E*TRADE Bank ($100 minimum)
1-800-ETBANK1
www.etrade.com

When you visit the E*TRADE web site, make sure to click into E*TRADE Bank to get information about the E*TRADE Bank Money Market Account Plus. E*TRADE Bank's money market account requires a $100 minimum opening deposit, but it allows unlimited ATM use and allows you to write three personal checks a month. You can also arrange for direct deposit of your paycheck. What's more, your funds are FDIC insured up to $100,000. If your balance drops below the $1,000 minimum, you get hit with a $10 fee, so be careful. Still, this is one of the easier low-minimum money market accounts to set up online or by phone.

Morgan Stanley ($1,000 to $5,000 minimum)
www.morganstanley.com

One of the world's largest full-service financial firms, Morgan Stanley offers a complete menu of brokerage services that includes numerous types of money market accounts. Depending on your advisor and account type, you will be required to deposit a minimum of $1,000 to $5,000. To be able to write checks, you need to make a $5,000 deposit. At this level, you can open Morgan Stanley's comprehensive full-service Active Assets Account (often called an "AAA" account). This account offers unlimited check writing, an ATM card, full-service brokerage, consolidated reporting, and a wonderful year-end summary report that shows all of your transactions for the year. You can also set up an automatic direct deposit or systematic investing plan with this account. Most full-service firms offer similar types of accounts, but the minimum deposit requirements are typically $10,000. (Morgan Stanley used to ask for that much, but they lowered it.) To open an account with Morgan Stanley, you need to visit a branch office. Visit their web site to locate a branch in your area or check the phone book.

Fidelity Investments ($2,500 minimum)
1-800-FIDELITY
www.fidelity.com

One of the leading providers of mutual funds and online brokerage accounts, Fidelity also has numerous branch locations that you can visit to get advice and transact business. Fidelity offers numerous money market accounts. You can open a basic money market account that allows check writing with a minimum deposit of just $2,500. They can mail you the forms to open this account, or you can visit one of their branches and do it face-to-face. They also allow for direct deposit and can accommodate a systematic investment plan.

Vanguard ($3,000 minimum)
1-877-662-7447
www.vanguard.com

Vanguard is known for offering one of the lowest cost and highest yielding money market accounts around. With an initial deposit of $3,000, you can open a basic money market account that allows you to write checks in the amount of $250 or more. Vanguard also allows direct deposit of your paycheck and can help you set up an automatic investment plan in which they debit your checking account. You can set up this account online or by mail.

Charles Schwab ($2,500)
1-866-855-9102
www.schwab.com

Charles Schwab has offices around the country as well as an easy-to-use web site. The minimum to open a money market account here is an initial deposit of $2,500.

PLAYING IT SAFE

Historically, money market accounts are considered to be among the safest investments around, virtually on a par with bank certificates of deposit. As of this writing, however, interest rates are at historic lows, and if they stay that way for a while, the banks and brokerage firms that offer them may find it increasingly difficult to make money on them.

Because of this, I strongly recommend investing only in established money market accounts at well-recognized, established financial institutions. Always ask how long the fund has been around, what kind of annualized return it generates, and what the expense ratio is (that is, what it costs the institution to run the fund). To really protect yourself, you might want to take a lower rate and go with a money market account that is federally insured.

GETTING AROUND THE MINIMUMS

Many brokerage firms may tell you that in order to open a money market account with them you need to make an initial deposit of at least $2,000. If that seems pretty steep to you, don't give up—there is often a way around it. Ask the brokerage if they offer a money market fund that takes systematic investments. Most do, and generally speaking, as long as you sign a form agreeing to make regular monthly investments, they'll let you open a brokerage account to invest in a money market fund with as little as $100. (Keep in mind, however, that if you open an account this way, you generally don't get check-writing privileges or an ATM card.)

NOW MAKE IT AUTOMATIC

Ultimately, you will want to keep your rainy day fund separate from your checking account. While you could put your rainy day money in the same account you use to pay your bills, you really shouldn't. When you keep your spending money and your emergency money in the same place, it's too easy to dip into the rainy day fund for monthly expenses— and before you know it, your emergency fund will be gone. So here's what I would do.

YOUR RAINY DAY FUND STEP BY STEP

1. Using the lists above as well as your own research, select a bank or brokerage that offers good money market rates, then open a money market account. If you've got more than $1,000 to deposit, you should be able to find a money market account that offers both check-writing privileges and an ATM card. (But, remember, don't use them unless it's an emergency.) If you don't have that much, then open a money market account without a check-writing option.

2. The best way to fund your rainy day account is to MAKE IT AUTOMATIC. To do this, first check to see if your employer will direct deposit your paycheck. (Again, all you have to do is contact your benefits office and ask if the company offers payroll direct deposit.) If they will, you can arrange to have all or part of your paycheck automatically deposited wherever you want. All your employer needs is your account number.

3. Decide how much you will save each month. My suggestion is that you strive to put at least 5 percent of your

net take-home pay in your rainy day account each month. Your employer will probably want you to specify an exact dollar amount, so do the math and indicate what it is.

4. If your employer won't do an automatic deposit into your money market account, arrange to have your checking account automatically fund your money market account. There are two ways to do this. Either you can instruct the bank where you have your checking account to transfer a specific dollar amount every two weeks to your money market account, or you can instruct the bank or brokerage firm that has your money market account to do what is called a systematic withdrawal from your checking account, in which money is automatically withdrawn from your checking account on a certain day each month and transferred into your money market account. Either way, everything is completely automated, and in most cases you should be able to make the arrangements online.

LET THE GOVERNMENT HELP!

I want to share one more really safe and simple way to automate your rainy day fund. The government has now made it incredibly easy to buy savings bonds online. If you are looking for a safe investment for your money that is guaranteed by the full faith and credit of the U.S. government, you may want to consider investing in U.S. savings bonds.

VISIT WWW.TREASURYDIRECT.GOV

The government's treasury direct web site www.treasurydirect.gov provides an incredibly easy way to invest as little as $50 a month automatically in two types of U.S. savings bonds, I-Bonds and EE Bonds, otherwise known as Inflation Bonds and Patriot Bonds. You can find the rates for both of these bonds by visiting this site and then clicking on "For EE/E Bond Investors" and "For I-Bond Investors."

ALL ABOUT INFLATION BONDS

I-Bonds are also known as Inflation Bonds. That's because their earnings rate is indexed to inflation. The return is calculated as a combination of a fixed rate of return and a semi-annual rate based on the consumer price index, so if inflation rears its ugly head again, the return on these bonds gets increased—and you get protected from being stuck with a low rate. (As of the writing of this book, the interest rate for I-Bonds was 4.80 percent.)

Other features of I-Bonds:
- Minimum purchase is just $50. (The maximum you can buy in a year is $30,000 worth.)
- Interest is generally added monthly.
- I-Bonds are sold at face value. What this means is that to buy $100 worth of I-Bonds costs you $100 in cash.
- I-Bonds earn interest for up to thirty years.
- You can sell an I-Bond after one year—although if you

sell before five years, you will be penalized three months' worth of interest. (This may seem like a stiff penalty, but given the good rates these bonds pay, it really isn't.)

ALL ABOUT PATRIOT BONDS

EE Bonds, also known as Patriot Bonds, are savings bonds that were issued following the September 11 terrorist attack. Their rate is calculated as 90 percent of the six-month average of the five-year Treasury Marketable Securities Yield. This sounds complicated, but all it means is that they pay 90 percent of the return you'd get from a five-year treasury note. As of early 2005, the EE Bond rate was 3.42 percent.

Features of Patriot Bonds:

- Interest is added monthly and compounded semiannually.
- EE Bonds are sold at 50 percent of the face value of the bond. What this means is that to buy $100 in Patriot Bonds, you actually fork over just $50. When the bonds come due after thirty years, you can cash them in for their full $100 face value.
- You can sell an EE Bond after owning it for just one year, and as with the I-Bond, if you sell before five years, you will lose the last three months of interest that you earned on the bond.

HOW TO AUTOMATE THE PURCHASE OF
SAVINGS BONDS

The government has made it really easy to automate your bond buying. Just go to **www.savingsbonds.gov** and click on the "Easy Saver Plan" button at the top of the page. This will jump you to a page that explains how to set up an automatic purchase plan for U.S. savings bonds.

The fact is that the government's Easy Saver Plan is tailor-made for Automatic Millionaires. Among other things, it lets you

- buy bonds with an automatic debit from your personal checking or savings account or using payroll deduction if your company offers it;
- set the account up online in minutes (or, if you want, download the forms to fill out and then mail or fax in);
- use a credit card to purchase bonds online twenty-four hours a day, seven days a week. (I don't recommend this option, but it is available.)

EITHER WAY, YOU WIN

You may now be wondering where I would put my rainy day money—in a money market account or in government savings bonds. They both have advantages. Money market accounts provide you with more liquidity (meaning you can get your hands on your money quickly and easily, without having to pay a penalty). But right now, at least, government savings bonds pay a higher rate of interest (because they are considered longer-term investments than money market accounts) and it's so easy to buy them automatically with a very small initial deposit. For many people, having both is a great option.

WHAT IF I'M IN DEBT?

If you owe credit card debt, then the order in which you do things should change. I recommend to people with big credit card balances that they build up just one month's worth of expenses in their security account and then concentrate on paying down their debt. Why? Because it doesn't make sense to have money earning 1 percent in a money market account at the same time that you're paying 20 percent on your credit card debt.

A bit later in this book you'll find a chapter on credit card debt. By the time you finish it, you'll know how to lower the interest rate on your credit cards faster—and get out of debt quicker—than most people.

But first let's find out the real secret to finishing rich while you're still young: becoming a homeowner.

AUTOMATIC MILLIONAIRE ACTION STEPS

Reviewing the steps we laid out in this chapter, here's what you should be doing right now to ensure yourself automatic financial security.

- ❑ Decide you're going to build an emergency cushion of cash (ideally, three months' or more worth of expenses).

- ❑ Decide you're going to earn interest on your savings (and make the most of your money).

- ❑ Open a rainy day money market account or set up a rainy day account by investing in U.S. savings bonds.

- ❑ Make your rainy day fund AUTOMATIC and let it grow until your emergency cushion is big enough for you to feel secure.

YOU ARE ALMOST DONE

It may seem hard to believe, but once you've made your future automatic and you've automated for a rainy day, you will be close to having your entire financial plan on automatic pilot.

Imagine never having to worry about money again! Well, that's what it's like to be an Automatic Millionaire—and that's what you are about to become.

CHAPTER SIX

AUTOMATIC DEBT-FREE HOMEOWNERSHIP

Of all the secrets to financial security that I share in this book, there are three that stand out in terms of importance and effectiveness. The first is to decide to Pay Yourself First 10 percent of your pretax income. The second is to Make It Automatic. The third is to . . .

BUY A HOME AND PAY IT OFF AUTOMATICALLY

In this chapter, we're going to look at why you should own your own home—and even more important, how you can pay for that home automatically so you can be debt-free before you're too old to enjoy it.

So let's get started.

Young or old, you want to own the place you live in. Why? It's simple. **You can't get rich renting.** As the old saying goes, landlords get rich and renters stay poor.

Think about it. As a renter, you can easily spend half a million dollars or more on rent over the years ($1,500 a month for thirty years comes to $540,000), and in the end wind up just where you started—owning nothing. Or you can buy a house and spend the same amount paying down a mortgage, and in the end wind up owning your own home free and clear!

The fact is, you aren't really in the game of building wealth until you own some real estate.

THE FIRST LANDLORD YOU SHOULD BECOME IS YOUR OWN

Study after study has shown that people who own their own homes wind up with an average net worth many times greater than that of those who rent. According to one survey of consumer finance published by the Federal Reserve in January 2003, the average net worth of renters was $4,800 vs. $171,700 for homeowners. In other words, homeowners were more than 31 times richer than renters!

But even more important than money is the feeling home-ownership gives you. When you own, you have the security that comes from knowing you are building equity and living in a place that belongs to you. You're not at the mercy of a landlord who can raise your rent or evict you.

So if you are currently renting, buying a place to live (whether it's a house or a condo) needs to be a priority. But can you really make buying a home and paying it off automatic and easy? The answer is yes, and this chapter will show you how.

DEBT-FREE HOMEOWNERSHIP MADE EASY

When I first met Jim and Sue McIntyre, one aspect of their story that really impressed me was how much they benefited from buying a house and paying it off early. If you remember, they bought their first home while they were still relatively young and, by doing nothing more complicated than accelerating their payments slightly, managed to pay off their thirty-year mortgage in less than twenty years. At that point, they rented out their first house for income and bought another home, which they also paid off in less than twenty years.

By the time the McIntyres reached their early fifties, they owned two homes completely free and clear. As a result, they were able to retire early—debt-free with close to a million dollars in real estate equity and positive cash flow.

We should all lead such lives. And the fact is, we can! Here's how.

STEP ONE: BUY A HOME

So you want to be a millionaire? Like I said before, there are only three things you really need to do: (1) decide to Pay Yourself First 10 percent of what you earn, (2) Make It Automatic, and (3) buy a home and pay it off early.

If you think there should be more to it than this, you're right. You have to be smart about how you do these things. As we've already seen, when it comes to Paying Yourself First, you've got to automate the process and make your investments with pretax dollars. It's the same when it comes to buying a home: You need to be smart about how you pay for it so you don't waste a fortune on financing. We'll be covering this in detail shortly. But first let's look at why buying a home is such a great deal.

SIX REASONS WHY HOMES MAKE GREAT INVESTMENTS

There are actually countless reasons why homes make great investments. Here are the top six.

1. Forced Savings.
Despite the impression you may get from the media, very few people actually lose their homes to foreclosure. According to the Mortgage Bankers Association of America, banks foreclose on less than 1.5 percent of residential mortgages. That's

because homeowners will do just about anything to keep from losing their homes. So one way of looking at home-ownership is as a kind of forced savings program, in which in order to keep your home, you must make a monthly contribution (in the form of a mortgage payment) to one of the best investments around—home equity.

2. Leverage.

One of the most effective financial tactics used by the really big wheeler-dealers is something called leverage—using borrowed money to multiply your potential gains. When you buy a home, you get to pay the leverage game too.

Here's how it works. Let's say you're buying a $250,000 home with a down payment of 20 percent. What this means is that you're putting in $50,000 of your own money and borrowing the remaining $200,000 from a bank. Since you've actually put in only one fifth of the purchase price, you've got five to one leverage. Now let's say the value of the house increases over the next five years to $300,000. Given that you've put in only $50,000, the $50,000 increase in value means you've effectively doubled your money. This is the power of leverage.

Over the last five years, many homes have doubled in price. Think what this means in terms of leverage. If you invested $50,000 in a $250,000 home five years ago and it's now worth $500,000, you've made $250,000 on a $50,000 investment. In investment circles, that's called a five-bagger—an amazing 500 percent return on your money.

3. OPM.

OPM stands for "other people's money." You hear this phrase a lot among smart investors. We discussed earlier how instead of working for their money, rich people get their money to work for them. Well, *really* rich people not only get their money to work for them but also get other people's money to work for them. When you buy a home, you are doing just that—using the bank's money to get rich. Meanwhile, your money can be working for you elsewhere—say, compounding in a retirement account.

4. Tax Breaks.

By letting you deduct the cost of the interest you pay on your mortgage (up to a maximum of $1 million), the government gives you a huge incentive to become a homeowner. The higher your tax bracket, the more the government is helping you buy a home. If you are in the 30 percent tax bracket, the government is basically subsidizing almost a third of your mortgage payment (particularly in the early years, when most of your monthly payment goes to pay interest).

5. Pride of Ownership.

When you own your own home, you own a piece of the American Dream. You put down roots, become part of a community, and enjoy the sense of pride that comes with ownership. This is more than just a warm, fuzzy feeling; it's something that gives you and your loved ones a real sense of security.

6. Real Estate Has Proven to Be a Great Investment.

For most people, the best investment they ever make is their home. (Ask your parents about this if they're homeowners.) But is this still true? As U.S. housing prices climbed steadily through the late 1990s and early years of the twenty-first century, some people began to worry if we were experiencing a real estate "bubble," similar to the unjustified run-up we saw with "dot-com" stocks. But homes are not stocks. They don't trade on an exchange. You can't buy and sell them with the click of a mouse. Yes, real estate values have been skyrocketing in value, and, yes, there have been some bad years and some bad times. But the bad times have always been temporary. Over the long run, real estate prices almost always go up, and buying a home almost always works out great. According to figures kept by the National Association of Realtors, there has never been a *national* real estate bubble. What's more, ever since 1968 (when they first started keeping records), real estate investments have averaged an annual return of 6.3 percent.

BUT WHAT ABOUT THE DOWN PAYMENT?

The number one reason people put off buying a home is because they think they can't afford it. More often than not, they are wrong.

In particular, would-be homebuyers are scared off by the down payment. People often think they need to come up with thousands if not tens of thousands of dollars in cash in order to get a mortgage. This is simply not true. There are all sorts of programs sponsored by developers, lenders, and even the government that can enable first-time homebuyers to finance as much as 95, 97, or even 100 percent of the purchase price. While borrowing so much can be risky (if you can't afford the monthly payments), it's also a way of getting out of a renting situation and into your own home much faster than saving up enough money to make a big down payment.

BILLIONS OF DOLLARS ARE AVAILABLE TO HELP YOU BUY

In 2002, President George W. Bush announced a goal of increasing the number of U.S. homeowners by 5.5 million over the next eight years. In order to make this happen, the government has earmarked billions of dollars to help first-time homebuyers handle their down payments. In addition, the government is also creating products to lower the overall cost of mortgages for first-time homebuyers.

AGENCIES AND COMPANIES THAT CAN HELP YOU BUY A HOME

U.S. Department of Housing and Urban Development
www.hud.gov

HUD's mission is to create opportunities for homeownership. To this end, it offers all kinds of assistance to would-be homebuyers, including grants to help people buy a first home. If you are a first-time homebuyer, visit this web site! It offers a wealth of resources on how to buy, what kind of help HUD offers, and how to qualify for assistance. You can even chat online with an agency representative and be referred to a housing counselor in your area.

National Council of State Housing Finance Agencies
www.ncsha.org

If you are a first-time homebuyer, you may qualify for special state loan programs specifically created to help people like you. The NCSHA web site contains links to housing finance agencies in every state, many of which offer programs that allow you to buy a home with a down payment of less than 5 percent. When you visit this site, click on the member list, then click to your state for contact information about your local housing finance agency. Call the agency directly and tell them you're a first-time homebuyer looking for a bank in your area that participates in the state housing loan program.

Fannie Mae
1-800-832-2345
www.fanniemae.com

The Federal National Mortgage Association, otherwise known as Fannie Mae, is a private company that operates under a congressional charter to increase the availability and affordability of homeownership for low-, moderate-, and middle-income Americans. Since 1968, Fannie Mae has helped 43 million families realize the dream of owning a home. In 2002, it created what it calls the American Dream Commitment, a program to provide $2 trillion in funding over the next decade in order to increase homeownership in America by 18 million new families. Fannie Mae doesn't lend money itself; what it does is provide the financing that makes it possible for banks to lend money to consumers. It also offers FREE reports that you are bound to find useful. *Opening the Door to a Home of Your Own, Choosing a Mortgage, Knowing Your Credit,* and *Borrowing Basics* are all available simply for the asking. Just call 1-800-688-4663 and they'll send you one or all of them. In addition, check out www.homepath.com, a related Fannie Mae web site that contains a consumer-friendly "For Home Buyers & Homeowners" section with helpful information on becoming a homeowner and finding a lender as well as additional resources.

Freddie Mac
1-800-373-3343
www.freddiemac.com

Since 1970, Freddie Mac (aka, the Federal Home Loan Mortgage Corporation) has financed 26 million homes in America—one out of every six built since it came into existence. Freddie Mac does not make loans to consumers; rather, it provides the financing that allows lenders to offer home loans that are affordable. The Freddie Mac web site is worth visiting—particularly the homebuyers section (at www.freddiemac.com/homebuyers), where you'll find a wonderful tool called "The Road to Home Ownership." Freddie Mac also has a related web site at www.homesteps.com, designed to help first-time homebuyers find a bargain on a home and get loan approval in one easy step. It does this by listing foreclosure auctions nationwide and providing information about loan programs that allow would-be homeowners to buy foreclosed properties with as little as 5 percent down.

LOAN PROGRAMS TO CONSIDER

FHA LOANS

The Federal Housing Administration (FHA) is an agency within HUD that provides lenders with mortgage insurance, thus giving them the security to lend to first-time homebuyers who otherwise might have trouble qualifying for a loan. In many cases, FHA loans can cover up to 97 percent of the purchase price and can be used to buy a second or third home. To get one, you need to work with a lender who is approved to do FHA loans. For more information, visit www.fhaloan.com. This web site is not run by the FHA, but it's a good place to start. (For referrals to FHA-approved lenders in your area, visit the HUD web site, www.hud.gov.)

VA LOANS

The U.S. Department of Veterans Affairs has a program that guarantees mortgage loans made to veterans of the U.S. armed services. The VA offers loans to both first- and second-time homebuyers. In addition to visiting the VA's own web site at www.va.gov, where you'll find a resource center and referrals to VA-approved lenders, you might also want to check out www.valoans.com. It's not run by the VA, but it is very useful nonetheless.

STATE BOND LOANS

Most states offer individual bond programs designed to help first-time homebuyers. Ask the manager or the mortgage specialist at your local bank for details. Also, as discussed above, visit the National Council of State Housing Finance Agencies web site (www.ncsha.org), for more information on these programs.

THE RENT YOU PAY TODAY COULD BUY YOU A HOME TOMORROW

Many people don't realize that the same amount of money they spend on rent today could buy them a home tomorrow. As of this writing (2005), interest rates continue to remain close to a forty-five-year low. They may be higher by the time you read this, but let's use the math we have at the moment. To put it simply, for every $1,000 you pay in monthly rent, you could support $125,000 worth of mortgage (including taxes and insurance). In other words, if your rent is currently $2,000 a month, you could afford to make payments on a $250,000 mortgage. In most parts of the country, that would buy you a lot of home!

HOW MUCH HOME CAN YOU AFFORD?

According to the FHA, a good rule of thumb is that most people can afford to spend 29 percent of their gross income on housing expenses—as much as 41 percent if they have no debt.

Annual Gross Income	Monthly Gross	29% of Gross	41% of Gross
$20,000	$1,667	$483	$683
$30,000	$2,500	$725	$1,025
$40,000	$3,333	$967	$1,367
$50,000	$4,176	$1,208	$1,712
$60,000	$5,000	$1,450	$2,050
$70,000	$5,833	$1,692	$2,391
$80,000	$6,667	$1,933	$2,733
$90,000	$7,500	$2,175	$3,075
$100,000	$8,333	$2,417	$3,417

As the table above indicates, if you earn $50,000 a year, you should be able to afford to spend at least $1,208 a month on housing—whether in the form of rent or mortgage payments. Keeping in mind that homeownership (buying) is better than home loanership (renting), check out the next table. It shows what the monthly payments would be for different amounts of 30-year-mortgages at different interest rates. (It doesn't include taxes or insurance; to figure them in, you'll need to check on what they run in your area.)

TYPICAL MORTGAGE PAYMENTS							
Monthly payments (principal and interest) for 30-year fixed rate mortgage. Taxes, insurance not included.							
Mortgage Amount	5.0%	5.5%	6.0%	6.5%	7.0%	7.5%	8.0%
$100,000	$537	$568	$600	$632	$668	$699	$734
$150,000	$805	$852	$899	$948	$998	$1,048	$1,100
$200,000	$1,074	$1,136	$1,199	$1,264	$1,331	$1,398	$1,468
$250,000	$1,342	$1,419	$1,499	$1,580	$1,663	$1,748	$1,834
$300,000	$1,610	$1,703	$1,799	$1,896	$1,996	$2,098	$2,201
$350,000	$1,879	$1,987	$2,098	$2,212	$2,329	$2,447	$2,568
$400,000	$2,147	$2,271	$2,398	$2,528	$2,661	$2,797	$2,935
$450,000	$2,415	$2,555	$2,698	$2,844	$2,994	$3,146	$3,302
$500,000	$2,684	$2,839	$2,998	$3,160	$3,327	$3,496	$3,665

THE KEY TO SUCCESS: GETTING THE FINANCING RIGHT

We've now come to the most important part of this chapter: how to pay off your home and become debt-free automatically. It's not enough just to buy a house. In fact, buying the house is often the easiest part. The real challenge comes in figuring out how you're going to pay for it. Indeed, the key to making it all work financially is getting the right kind of mortgage.

There are many types of mortgages. Each type has its advantages and disadvantages. Let's take a look at what is available, and then I'll share my recommendation for how an Automatic Millionaire should select a mortgage.

WEB SITES TO HELP YOU FIND AND FINANCE A HOME

www.citimortgage.com
www.eloan.com
www.homebuying.about.com
www.homebuyingguide.org
www.homepath.com
www.lendingtree.com
www.pueblo.gsa.gov
www.quickenloan.com
www.realtor.com
www.smartmoney.com/home/buying
www.wellsfargo.com

MORTGAGE TYPES

30-YEAR FIXED RATE

Features	Pro	Con	Whom is this mortgage right for?
"Vanilla" mortgage rate stays the same for the 30-year life of loan.	Locks in your interest rate and protects you if rates rise. Payments are the same each month. Easy to track and monitor.	You are locked into a rate for 30 years unless you refinance.	If you are conservative and plan on being in your home a long time (at least 7 to 10 years), this offers the most benefits and flexibility.

15-YEAR FIXED RATE

Features	Pro	Con	Whom is this mortgage right for?
Similar to 30-year mortgage, except the rate and mortgage are for 15 years.	The rate on a 15-year is lower than that on a 30-year. You pay off your home and become debt-free in 15 years. Also easy to track and monitor.	The monthly mortgage payment is higher than with a 30-year mortgage.	If you are a really committed saver and plan to live in your home longer than 10 years, this is a great loan. You can lock in a rate and be debt-free in a decade and a half.

SHORT-TERM ADJUSTABLE RATE (5 YEARS OR LESS)			
Features	**Pro**	**Con**	**Whom is this mortgage right for?**
Interest rates may be fixed for 6 months to a year. Some of these mortgages have rates that change monthly.	You get a substantial break on the interest rate, so the monthly payment will be much less with this mortgage than with any other loan.	If interest rates go up quickly, you can find yourself having trouble making the payments.	These loans are typically used by people who want to keep their monthly payments as low as possible. They make most sense for those who can handle risk and don't expect to live in the house more than a few years. A great deal if rates stay low.

INTERMEDIATE ADJUSTABLE RATE (OFTEN CALLED A 3/1, 5/1, 7/1, OR 10/1 ARM)			
Features	**Pro**	**Con**	**Whom is this mortgage right for?**
Interest rate locks in for a specific period and then adjusts annually or every six months based on the going rates.	Relatively low rates.	Your rate is locked only for a limited time. If rates rise, your monthly mortgage payment rises.	Great for a person looking for low rates and lower monthly payments who's not planning on keeping the property very long. The longer you lock in the rate, the higher the payments and the lower the risk.

WHY A 30-YEAR MORTGAGE CAN MAKE SENSE

So which type of mortgage would I select? My first choice for most people is a 30-year fixed rate mortgage. Why? Well, to begin with, they are simple. They're also a great deal when interest rates are low, since they lock in that low rate for the next 30 years.

What's a low rate? Historically, anything below 8 percent is considered to be very low. In 2005, 30-year mortgage rates were below 6 percent. To get a quick look at where rates are right now, visit any of the web sites listed on page 173 or check your local newspaper.

My favorite places on the web to go to review mortgage rates are www.eloan.com and www.yahoo.com (click on "Finance" and then click through to "Loans" and "Rates"). Both sites are easy to use and allow you to do searches for rates without having to provide personal information. Two other good places to visit for mortgage-rate information are www.lendingtree.com and www.quickenloan.com.

HOW YOU CAN GET RIPPED OFF BY A 30-YEAR MORTGAGE

One great thing about 30-year mortgages is that they lock in a rate for 30 years. Another great thing is that it's relatively easy to carry them. After all, the monthly payments on a 30-

year are lower than they are on, say, a 15-year mortgage. Still, most people get burned on their 30-year mortgages. That's because you don't actually want to pay for your home for more than 30 years. Why? Because if you do, you'll be in debt and paying off your home forever.

Unfortunately, 30-year mortgages end up being more profitable for the bank than for you. The math is simple. Say you buy a home for $250,000. If you get a typical 30-year mortgage at 8 percent, your mortgage payments over the 30 years will wind up totaling about $660,000. Think about that. You bought a $250,000 home and it actually cost you $660,000! Where did the extra $410,000 go? It went to pay the interest on your mortgage—which is to say it went into the bank's pocket, not into your house.

What makes 30-year mortgages more of a problem for most people is that most people live in their homes for less than ten years. The average is only about five to seven years. Now, if you live in a house for, say, seven years and then sell it, you will have paid down the principal on your mortgage by only about 4 percent! That's right. On average, **during the first ten years of your loan, more than 90 percent of your payments go to pay interest.** What it means is that tens of millions of Americans with 30-year mortgages are wasting a fortune paying for their homes in this way.

HOW TO SAVE YOURSELF A DECADE'S WORTH OF WORK

It's hard to get debt-free—never mind rich—when virtually all of your mortgage payment is going to pay bank interest. Yet that is what happens for the first ten years of most 30-year mortgages. To put it another way, with a mortgage like that, you spend the first ten years working hard for the bank but building little equity for yourself.

But there is an alternative. If you follow the system I'm about to share with you, you could save yourself nearly a decade's worth of work.

THE SECRET SYSTEM TO DEBT-FREE HOMEOWNERSHIP

The secret to being an Automatic Millionaire is keeping it simple. So here's what you do. Find yourself that home you want and buy it. Get a 30-year mortgage and then use my secret system.

What's the secret system? It's using a biweekly payment plan to pay down your mortgage, and doing it all automatically.

What's a biweekly payment plan? Glad you asked. Keep reading . . .

THE AUTOMATIC MILLIONAIRE BIWEEKLY MORTGAGE PAYMENT PLAN

Anyone can do this. You don't need a special mortgage. All you need is your mortgage. What you do is take the normal 30-year mortgage you have, and instead of making the monthly payment the way you normally do, you split it down the middle and pay half every two weeks.

Let's do some more simple math. Say your mortgage payment is $2,000 a month. Normally, you would pay this amount once a month. But not anymore. Starting next month, you are going to begin sending your mortgage lender $1,000 every two weeks. By doing this, something miraculous will happen. Depending on your interest rate, you can end up paying off your mortgage early—somewhere between five and ten years early! (The average is about seven years.)

Do you have any idea how much money you can save by paying off your mortgage early? Once again, it depends on your interest rate, but on average a U.S. homeowner can save upwards of $100,000 over the life of his or her mortgage just by following this simple program. And if that's not enough incentive, think about being debt-free and potentially ready to retire up to ten years sooner than you'd planned!

WHY THIS WORKS

What happens when you make a payment every two weeks instead of once a month is that you end up making one extra month's worth of mortgage payments each year. (By paying half of your monthly payment every two weeks, over the course of a year you will make 26 half-payments—the equivalent of 13 full payments, or one more payment than there are months in a year.)

I said before that this was a secret system. To be honest, it's not really a secret anymore. Lenders have known about it for years, and recently the media has picked up on it. Like Pay Yourself First, it's a tactic people may know about but don't actually use.

THE $119,000 DIFFERENCE

As the following amortization schedule shows, using a monthly payment plan to pay off a $250,000 30-year mortgage with an interest rate of 8 percent will cost you a total of $410,388.12 in interest charges over the life of the loan. On a biweekly basis, the same mortgage will cost you a total of just $291,226.69 in interest. In others words, switching to the biweekly plan will save you more than $119,000.

To find the calculator that produced this amortization table so you can plug in your own numbers (for free), go online and visit www.bankrate.com. First, click on "Calculators," then "Mortgages," and then "Get a biweekly mortgage payment plan." This will take you to the best free calculator I've found on the Internet. You can quickly run the numbers for your own mortgage and see in black and white why it makes sense to switch to a biweekly payment plan.

MONTHLY PAYMENTS VS. BIWEEKLY PAYMENTS		

Principal=**$250,000**   Interest Rate=**8.00%**   Term=**30** years

Monthly Payment: **$1,834.41**	Biweekly Payment: **$917.21**
Average Interest **$1,139.97** vs.	Average Interest **$372.41**
Each Month	Each Biweekly Period

Total Interest: **$410,388.12**   Total Interest: **$291,226.69**

Year	Principal Balance (Monthly Payments)	Principal Balance (Biweekly Payments)
1	$247,911.59	$245,930.37
2	$245,649.84	$241,523.53
3	$243,200.37	$236,751.55
4	$240,547.60	$231,584.16
5	$237,674.64	$225,988.62
6	$234,563.23	$219,929.44
7	$231,193.58	$213,368.21
8	$227,544.25	$206,263.32
9	$223,592.02	$198,569.74
10	$219,311.76	$190,238.67
11	$214,676.24	$181,217.31
12	$209,655.98	$171,448.45
13	$204,219.03	$160,870.16
14	$198,330.82	$149,415.36
15	$191,953.90	$137,011.44
16	$185,047.69	$123,579.76
17	$177,568.27	$109,035.14
18	$169,468.06	$93,285.38
19	$160,695.54	$76,230.62
20	$151,194.91	$57,762.73

Year	Principal Balance (Monthly Payments)	Principal Balance (Biweekly Payments)
21	$140,905.72	$37,764.62
22	$129,762.54	$16,109.50
23	$117,694.48	$ 0.00
24	$104,624.78	$ 0.00
25	$90,470.30	$ 0.00
26	$75,141.00	$ 0.00
27	$58,539.38	$ 0.00
28	$40,559.83	$ 0.00
29	$21,087.99	$ 0.00
30	$0.00	$ 0.00
Result:	Paid off in 30 years	Paid off in 23 years

HOW TO SET THIS UP

To set up a biweekly payment plan, all you need to do is call your lender (the bank that holds your mortgage). Tell them that starting next Friday you want to start paying your mortgage on a biweekly basis and so you want to know if they offer a biweekly mortgage payment plan. Remember, this does not mean that you are refinancing or changing your mortgage. All it means is that you are interested in signing up for a service to pay off your mortgage in a slightly different manner—namely, one that will allow you to make your mortgage payments on a biweekly basis. There's a good chance your bank or the company that holds your loan offers just such a program. (At Wells Fargo, for example, it's called "Equity En-hancer.")

Here are some of the powerful benefits of an automatic biweekly mortgage payment plan:

- It saves you thousands of dollars in interest payments (maybe hundreds of thousands).
- It puts you on a forced savings system.
- It makes your cash flow easier (because you pay your mortgage every time you get paid).
- You'll never have to worry about paying your mortgage late because it's automated.
- It cuts years off your mortgage!

ALL IT TAKES IS FIVE MINUTES

Setting up one of these programs yourself is pretty darn easy. If your mortgage is with one of the larger banks, they will probably refer you to an outside company that runs the pro-gram for them. For a one-time set-up fee of $195 to $395, plus a nominal transfer charge that (depending on the com-pany you use) ranges from $2.50 to $6.95 every two weeks when they automatically move your money from your check-ing account to your mortgage account, this outside company will totally automate the process for you.

WHAT TO WATCH OUT FOR

A lot of companies now provide these services. I recommend that you try to use one that is referred to you by your bank. That way you can be reasonably sure you're dealing with a reputable firm. One of the biggest such firms is a company called **Paymap Inc.** It currently provides this service for more than thirty financial institutions, including six of the nation's seven largest banks. As of the writing, Paymap charges a setup fee of $295 and $2.50 per transaction. They call their program Equity Accelerator®. (You can contact Paymap directly at www.paymap.com or by calling 1-800-209-9700 to see if they can help you.)

WHAT TO ASK

The three most important questions to ask a service company before you sign up for their biweekly mortgage plan are these:

- What do you do with my money when you get it?
- When do you actually fund the extra payments toward my mortgage?
- How much will it cost me to use the program?

These three questions are critical, and here's why. Some companies hang on to the extra money you're putting toward your mortgage and actually send it to your mortgage holder in a lump sum once a year. That's not what you want. You want a company that makes extra payments to your mortgage as soon as possible. This way your extra payments are paying down your mortgage faster. You also want to understand how the costs involved compare to the savings you will realize so you can make an informed decision.

HOW CAN I JUST DO THIS MYSELF?

Logic would tell you that you should be able to set up a program like this yourself. Unfortunately, you can't. If you split your monthly mortgage payment in half and send it in every two weeks, the bank will just send it back to you because they won't know what to do with it. Just to be sure, you can call your bank and ask, but in my experience they say, "Nope."

ISN'T THIS EXPENSIVE?

Let's do the math. If you're paying $2.50 per transfer every two weeks, that comes to roughly $65 a year. Over twenty-two years it totals just over $1,430, not including the set-up fee. Figure that the transfer fee will probably go up a little over time, and there's no question that a biweekly mortgage system will cost you thousands of dollars.

So why do it? The answer is that the few thousand dollars you're spending will save you tens of thousands of dollars, if not more. In the simple example I used on pages 180–82, you would have saved more than $119,000 over the life of the mortgage. Assuming you found the most expensive company out there to do this and spent $10,000 to run this program over twenty-two years, you're still ahead some $109,000. More realistically, with a company like PayMap, you would spend closer to $2,000 and save $117,000.

Now, trust me on this. Many people will go crazy when

they read this. They will get all up in arms about what a terrible idea it is to spend what amounts to the cost of one dinner at McDonald's a month to have their mortgage completely automated and set up so they can be debt-free almost a decade ahead of schedule. These people are being penny-wise and dollar-foolish. They will be missing the point—which is that by setting up a biweekly mortgage payment program, you can create in just a few minutes a simple, completely automated system that will free you of debt much earlier than you otherwise would be, bringing you that much closer to being an Automatic Millionaire. And not only that, but as a value-added service, the companies that run biweekly payment programs often review your mortgage statements annually to check for mistakes your bank may make in crediting your mortgage. This is a tremendous service. Whether or not you make extra payments, always watch your mortgage like a hawk! Banks make mistakes all the time crediting mortgage payments—and if they are not caught, these mistakes can cost you big money.

TWO SIMPLE WAYS TO ACCOMPLISH THE SAME THING AT NO COST

Okay, so you listened to my argument and you are still thinking that you don't want to spend the money. You like the idea of being debt-free early and automatically, but you want dinner at McDonald's this month and you don't want to spend money to set this up.

I understand. I happen to love McDonald's. Seriously, don't worry about it. Here are two simple ways to accomplish almost the exact same thing **without paying a fee.**

NO-FEE APPROACH NO. I

Whatever your mortgage payment happens to be, just add 10 percent to it each month. For instance, using the example on pages 180–82, let's say your monthly payment is $1,834. Ten percent of that is $183. If you paid exactly $183 a month extra on that mortgage each month (that is, instead of sending the bank $1,834, you sent them $2,017), you would end up paying off your home in twenty-two years—saving approximately $129,000 over the life of the mortgage. To run this calculation yourself, go to www.bankrate.com and click on "Calculator," then "Mortgages," and then on "Mortgage Calculator." If you don't want to do this yourself, simply call your bank and tell them you are interested in paying an extra 10 percent toward your mortgage and you'd like them to mail or fax you an amortization schedule. They should be willing to do this for free in just a few minutes. Given the lack of set-up costs and transfer fees with this approach, you should wind up saving about $15,000 more than you would with the biweekly mortgage plan.

Once again, the key to making this work is Making It Automatic. If you're like most people, chances are you won't write a check for 110 percent of your mortgage payment every time—not if it's left up to you each month. Regardless of what's going on in your life at the time, you'll always be able to come up with a good reason why this isn't a good month to make the extra payment.

The way to avoid this trap is to Make It Automatic. Arrange to have your mortgage payment transferred from your checking account automatically.

NO-FEE APPROACH NO. 2

Whatever your mortgage payment happens to be, simply pick one month a year to pay your mortgage bill twice. That is, send the bank one extra payment a year. My suggestion is that you do this in May or June—hopefully just after you've received your tax refund. Whatever month you choose, don't just send the bank a check for double the normal amount. This will confuse them. Instead, write two checks for the regular monthly amount. Send one in with your mortgage coupon as always and send the other with a note explaining that you want the entire amount applied to your principal. This will give you the same cost savings as the 10 percent extra plan, with no extra charges.

ALL THINGS BEING EQUAL . . .

Truth be told, while these no-fee approaches will work, in the real world very few people will actually make the required extra payments, whether they are once a year or once a month. So here's my recommendation. Decide if you want someone else to do this for you or if you want to handle it yourself. If you want help, first reach out to your bank and see whom they refer you to and look at the cost involved, and also call PayMap, the company I discussed on page 184, for a comparison. Have the companies send you all the information they have on their biweekly mortgage payment plans and then READ IT. Even if you don't use their service, you'll understand more about the power of paying down a mortgage early. Think through if the added cost is worth it for you to completely automate paying your home off early.

If you decide not to go this route, then I would recommend that you try the first no-fee option: paying an extra 10 percent on your monthly mortgage payment. You can automate the extra payment simply by increasing the size of the automatic transfer you arrange between your checking account and your mortgage lender each month.

QUESTIONS TO ASK YOUR BANK

Whichever route you take, there are a couple of questions you should ask your bank or mortgage company first.

Can I make extra payments on my mortgage without penalty?

The answer should be yes. (You should never sign up for a mortgage that charges a prepayment penalty.)

If I send in extra money beyond my required mortgage payment, what do I need to do to make SURE the extra payment is used to pay down my principal?

YOU MUST ASK THIS QUESTION! Amazingly enough,

standard operating procedure at most banks is to take extra payments and hold them in a non-interest-bearing account—not use them to pay down your mortgage. The bank will probably tell you that you need to send them a letter specifically requesting that your extra payment be applied to the principal. (Ask them if they have a form letter to this effect that you can sign.) Some banks may even ask you to send them the extra payment (that additional 10 percent) separately. If you've automated your mortgage payments, this should be no big deal. Your bank would simply automate two fund transfers a month on the same day.

WHAT IF I PLAN TO LIVE IN MY HOME LESS THAN THIRTY YEARS?

Earlier, I pointed out that average homeowners live in their home less than ten years. So why should you bother trying to pay off your mortgage early if you're probably going to sell your house and move?

The answer is automated forced savings. The faster you pay down your mortgage, the faster you build equity in your home. When you sell your home, you cash out that equity. At that point, you can either use it to help you buy a new home with a smaller mortgage or use it to increase your savings. Either is great.

TAKE ADVANTAGE OF BIWEEKLY
MORTGAGES

Some banks don't encourage these payment plans. Why? The basic reason is obvious: money! Banks make a lot more money on a loan if you pay it off over thirty years as opposed to, say, twenty.

There are other reasons as well. When you make extra payments, the bank has to handle your money more often than it would if it were paying only once a month. This increases their operating costs. But that's their problem, not yours. As an Automatic Millionaire, your concern is saving money and speeding to the day when you are debt-free. That's why the biweekly mortgage payment plan or simply paying a little extra each month makes sense. This one idea, if implemented properly, can return the investment you made in this book about 6,000 times over. More important, it can make you richer faster and able to retire sooner. **Proof once again that information is power when you use it.**

AUTOMATIC MILLIONAIRE ACTION STEPS

Here's what you should be doing right now to become a debt-free homeowner . . . automatically.

❏ If you don't already own your home, make the decision to become a homeowner.

❏ Go to www.eloan.com and calculate how much you can afford to spend on a home.

❏ Go to www.bankrate.com and use its calculator to see how much you can save by making your mortgage payments biweekly.

❏ Decide to pay off your mortgage early by using the biweekly mortgage payment plan, or by making payments yourself and adding something extra, either each month or once a year.

❏ If you are interested in a biweekly payment plan, contact your bank and ask them if they offer such programs or can refer you to a company that does.

❏ Whatever you decide to do with your mortgage payment, MAKE IT AUTOMATIC.

Now that you've learned the secret to debt-free homeownership, let's find out how to overcome the one remaining hurdle that keeps most people from getting rich: the deadly financial trap of credit card debt.

CHAPTER SEVEN

THE AUTOMATIC DEBT-FREE LIFESTYLE

For most of us, debt can be a trap that forces us to work longer than we should have to. What puts us into debt are bad habits such as running up big balances on our credit cards and then paying them down slowly, if at all. You can be hurt and held down by habits like these, or you can take action to break them. One of the most important lessons in this book is that Automatic Millionaires don't do debt.

In this chapter, you are going to learn a series of concrete steps that will enable you to regain control over your credit cards and stay out of debt in the future. If you don't happen to have any credit card debt, you should still read this chapter because it will motivate you to stay debt-free.

BORROW MONEY TO MAKE MONEY, NOT TO LOSE IT

One reason Jim and Sue McIntyre always avoided credit card debt was that they were raised by very old-school, Depression-era parents. If you know anyone who lived through the Great Depression of the 1930s, you may have heard their stories about what it felt like to have total poverty everywhere. There were no jobs. People had no money.

While some stores offered credit to good customers, credit cards as we know them today didn't exist. What this meant was that if you didn't have any money, you were in trouble. As a result, people who lived through the Depression came out of it with an intense dislike of being in debt and a powerful belief in the importance of saving. Ask any survivor of the Depression what they think about debt, and I'll bet the answer you get is similar to this: The only time borrowing makes sense is when you do it to buy something that can go up in value (like a home).

TELL THE TRUTH: ARE YOU BIG HAT, NO CATTLE?

People in Texas have a great way of describing someone who tries to look like more than he really is. They call him a "big hat, no cattle" guy.

In other words, he may look like a wealthy rancher, but in

fact there's no ranch, no cattle, no nothing. Just a big hat (and probably a fancy car).

Every day, I meet people who look rich. You probably meet them too. They have nice clothes, drive nice cars, and sometimes even live in nice homes. But when you peel back their finances, what you find is that they don't own what they wear or drive or live in. It's all rented or paid for with plastic. All they really have is a heaping mound of credit card debt.

What about you?

THE AVERAGE AMERICAN FAMILY OWES $8,400 IN CREDIT CARD DEBT

Try this hat on for size.

All told, Americans currently owe about half a trillion dollars in credit card debt. (That's just credit card debt, mind you—it doesn't include car loans, mortgages, or other debts.) That works out to be about $8,400 per household.

WHY MOST AMERICANS WILL BE PAYING OFF THEIR CREDIT CARDS FOR THE REST OF THEIR LIVES

Now, what do you think most people do when their credit card bill arrives every month? If you said they pay the minimum amount due, you're right.

Guess how much it will end up costing you to pay off an $8,400 balance on a credit card that charges 18 percent interest if you pay only the minimum each month?

The answer is $20,615! But wait—it's really worse than that.

AT THIS RATE, YOU'LL BE PAYING OFF YOUR BALANCE FOR THIRTY YEARS!

If you pay just the minimum due each month on an $8,400 credit balance, you will wind up having to make 365 monthly payments before it goes to zero. That's thirty years and five months' worth of payments. And that's assuming you never charge another dime on the card, never get hit with a late fee, and are never billed for an annual service fee.

Can you imagine it? Thirty years and five months' worth of payments—and that's for a card that charges 18 percent annual interest. Many cards charge much higher rates—some as high as 29 percent.

Here's the bottom line: You cannot become an Automatic Millionaire if you run up credit card balances and pay only the minimum due. All you'll accomplish doing that is making the credit card company rich while you stay poor.

HOW ONE DAY OF SHOPPING CAN TAKE THIRTEEN YEARS TO PAY OFF

The most dangerous thing about credit card debt may be how easy it is to get sucked in. Take the common practice many retailers follow of offering you a discount if you agree to sign up for a store charge card. Here's how it works. Imagine you're at the local outlet of a national clothing chain and you've picked out $1,100 worth of new outfits (let's say three shirts, two sweaters, a pair of pants or a dress, and a pair of shoes). While ringing up your purchase, a really nice, chipper, good-looking salesperson will smile at you and ask, "Wouldn't you like to save 10 percent on your purchase today? You know, you could save more than a hundred dollars by opening up one of our charge accounts. It will only take a minute."

A typical shopper, trying to be smart, will think, *Oh, great—I save a hundred dollars! Let's do it!*

Now, imagine that when the bill arrives, you make the minimum payment due—which is exactly what the store hopes will happen. If the interest rate is 18 percent, the $1,000 balance will take you 153 payments—or nearly thirteen years—to pay off. By then, the clothes will be long gone and you will have paid more than $2,100 for your $1,000 purchase.

It's a great deal for the store and a really terrible one for you.

So here is my suggestion for what you should do when the chipper salesperson asks if you want to earn yourself a discount by signing up for a store credit card.

JUST SAY NO

Repeat after me.

No.

No, I don't want a credit card.

No, I don't want a 10 percent discount.

No, I don't want six months' free interest.

No.

NO.

NO!

HOW MUCH DO YOU OWE?

By now I hope you are highly motivated to get out of debt and stay out.

So here's the question. Do you have credit card debt?

YES, I'VE GOT IT . . . BUT NOT FOR LONG

I have _____ [insert number] credit cards in my name.

My spouse/partner has _____ credit cards in his/her name.

My children (or other dependents) have _____ credit cards in their names.

The current outstanding balance owed on all these credit cards is $_____.

The average interest rate we're paying on these balances is _____%.

BEWARE OF THE "QUICK FIX"

It's important to be realistic about credit card debt. You are not going to be able to solve your problems overnight. It probably took a long time to get into trouble with credit card debt. And chances are it will take you a long time to get out of it.

With this in mind, you should be suspicious of so-called experts who claim they can solve all your credit problems with some magical quick fix. If you are drowning in debt, there are reputable credit-counseling firms that can help you come up with a plan to pay off your debts. One of the most highly regarded referral services is Consumer Credit Counseling Services.

CCCS is an offshoot of the National Foundation for Credit Counseling, the nation's oldest national nonprofit organization for consumer counseling and education on budgeting, credit, and debt resolution. It has more than 1,300 local affiliates around the nation. You can find one near you by telephoning 301-589-5600 or by going online to www.nfcc.org.

When you contact Consumer Credit Counseling Services, you will be referred to a nonprofit credit counseling group in your area that can help you. When you call to arrange a meeting with this group, try to find out as much as you can about what they can and can't do to help you. One important question to ask is whether using their services will hurt your credit rating. And before you sign on with anyone, check with the local chapter of the Better Business Bureau to see if they have any complaints logged against them.

OPERATION "NO MORE DEBT"

Okay, let's get down to the tools. There are five concrete steps you should take to get out of credit card debt and stay out.

STEP ONE **STOP DIGGING**

Let's start with the basics. If you are in a credit card hole—meaning you have credit card debt and you want to get rid of it—then you need to stop digging.

What does this mean? Well, in order to stop digging yourself deeper into the hole, it probably would make sense to throw away your shovel. In other words, get rid of your credit cards. After all, a person who wants to get out of credit card debt but carries credit cards in his wallet is like an alcoholic who wants to stop drinking but carries a bottle of vodka around with him.

I speak from experience here. I used to have a huge problem with credit card debt. (When I was in college, I racked up more than $10,000 in credit card charges buying clothing, furniture, stereo equipment, and other things I didn't really need and couldn't really afford.) After trying all kinds of self-control exercises, I discovered that the only one that worked was to STOP GOING SHOPPING WITH CREDIT CARDS IN MY POCKET.

STEP TWO RENEGOTIATE THE INTEREST RATE ON YOUR DEBT

Once you've acted to prevent things from getting any worse, you can start trying to make your current situation better. The basic goal here is to make paying off your credit card balance as easy as possible. The easiest and most effective way to do this is to get your credit card company to lower the interest rate it charges you.

Here's what you need to do in order to accomplish this.

1. Find out how much interest you are paying.

Pull out your credit card statements and read the fine print. What's the interest rate you are currently paying on your balance? If you find it difficult to figure this out, call the company and ask them exactly how much your debt is costing you. Tell them you want to know the effective rate, not the rate above prime. They will understand this question and by law they have to answer truthfully.

2. Ask for a lower rate.

Once you've found out the interest rate you're currently paying, tell the credit card company it's too high and you'd like them to lower it. (Do this with all the credit card accounts you have.) If the company says no, tell them that you will be closing your account this week and transferring your balance to a competitor who offers better rates. So there's no doubt about your seriousness, tell them the name of the competitor you have in mind. (It shouldn't be difficult to come up with a name, since you're probably constantly getting applications in the mail from credit card companies who want you to transfer your balances to them.) By the way, don't waste time by discussing interest rates with the first customer representative who takes your call. Ask to speak with a supervisor. Supervisors have the authority to give you a lower rate right then and there on the phone. In many cases, you can cut your rate in half simply by asking; you can even get them to waive the annual fee for your card.

3. Consolidate your debt.

If you have several credit cards, a really effective way to make it easier to get out of debt is to consolidate all of your balances on just one card. Again, all you need to do is "just ask." When you are negotiating with the credit card companies to lower your interest rate, tell them that you're prepared to move all your credit card debt to the company that offers you the lowest rate. What's low? Well, smart negotiators always do some research first. In this case, go online to www.bankrate. com or lowermybills.com, or check the business section of your local newspaper. See what the national average is for credit card rates—and ask for half of that. Even better, ask the credit card company what it is offering to customers like you who are willing to consolidate their debt. Let them try to sell you! You may find that in order to get all of your business, one of your credit card companies will offer to waive all interest charges for six months. If so, be careful—ask them what the rate will be in the seventh month, and remember it! It may jump to 25 percent in which case you will need to move once again to new card company. Of course, the game here is not credit card debt shuffling. It's finding the lowest rate you can, and then following the next three steps to get yourself out of debt completely.

STEP THREE PAY FOR THE PAST; PAY FOR THE FUTURE

Earlier, we saw how the kind of wealth you will build is determined by the way cash flows through your life. With that in mind, I suggested you make it a goal to Pay Yourself First 10 percent of your pretax income. However, if you have credit card debt, you need a different plan.

Here's what I suggest for people with credit card debt. Whatever amount you decide to Pay Yourself First, split it in half, with 50 percent going to you and 50 percent going to pay off your debt.

For example, let's say you earn $50,000 a year and have decided to Pay Yourself First 10 percent of your pretax income. Normally, this would mean you'd be putting aside $5,000 a year, or $416 a month, for yourself. But if you have credit card debt, you split the $416 a month in half, putting aside $208 a month for yourself and $208 a month to debt reduction.

The reason I suggest splitting your Pay Yourself First money in this way is so you can make progress on your future while you are getting yourself out of debt. The rationale here is as much emotional as it is financial. By doing both of these things at the same time, you will feel your progress. You'll see money being saved and debt being reduced.

If you were to direct all of your available cash flow to debt reduction, with the idea that you wouldn't begin to save until all your credit card bills were paid off, it might literally be years before you could begin saving for the future. This is too negative—so negative, in fact, that many people who follow this path get discouraged, give up early, and never get to the saving part.

I call my system "Bury the past and jump to the future." Try it. It works.

STEP FOUR DOLP YOUR DEBT OUT OF EXISTENCE

As I described above, the easiest and most efficient way of getting out of credit card debt is to consolidate all your balances in one account and then, as I suggested in Step Three, use half your Pay Yourself First money to pay it down. But what do you do if for some reason (say, you owe so much that no company will give you a sufficient credit limit) you can't consolidate your debt?

The answer is to DOLP™ your way out of debt.

I first described the DOLP system in *The Finish Rich Workbook*. The basic idea is to rid yourself of credit card debt once and for all by paying off all your balances and then closing all your credit card accounts.

In other words, your credit cards are all going to be Dead On Last Payment—or DOLP, for short.

Of course, when you have a lot of credit cards, figuring out how to pay them all off can be pretty daunting. Do you pay a little on all of them at once? Or should you concentrate on one card at a time? And if so, which one goes first?

This is where the DOLP system comes in.

Here's what you do.

- Make a list of the current outstanding balances on each of your credit card accounts.
- Divide each balance by the minimum payment that particular card company wants from you. The result is that account's DOLP number. For example, say your outstanding Visa balance is $500 and the minimum payment due is $50. Dividing the total debt ($500) by the minimum payment ($50) gives you a DOLP number of 10.
- Once you've figured out the DOLP number for each account, rank them in reverse order, putting the account with the lowest DOLP number first, the one with the second lowest number second, and so on. The table on the next page shows what your list should look like.

Account	Outstanding Balance	Monthly Minimum Payment	DOLP (Outstanding Balance divided by Monthly Minimum Payment)	DOLP Ranking (Lowest DOLP number is ranked #1)
Visa	$500	$50	10	1
MasterCard	$775	$65	12	2
Sears card	$1,150	$35	33	3

You now know the most efficient order in which you should pay off your various credit card balances. Take half your Pay Yourself First money and apply it to the card with the lowest DOLP number. For each of your other cards, you make only the minimum payment.

In the example above, the card with the lowest DOLP number is Visa. So each month, you'd devote half your Pay Yourself First amount to reducing your Visa balance, while making the minimum payments on the other cards. Once you've DOLPed your Visa account (that is, paid it off entirely), you'd close it down and turn your attention to the card with the next lowest DOLP ranking—in this case, MasterCard.

You should continue doing this until you've DOLPed your way to being debt-free.

Here's a blank table you can fill in to create your own DOLP list.

Account	Outstanding Balance	Monthly Minimum Payment	DOLP (Outstanding Balance divided by Monthly Minimum Payment)	DOLP Ranking (Lowest DOLP number is ranked #1)

STEP FIVE NOW MAKE IT AUTOMATIC!

Setting up an automatic payment plan for your credit card debt is easy. Simply call your credit card company and tell them you would like to arrange for them to make an automatic debit from your checking account each month. If they can't do that, then check with your bank and see if they offer online bill-paying services that allow you to arrange to have money automatically transferred from your checking account to your credit card company on a specific date each month. As I explained above, the amount of the debit should be one half of whatever you've decided to Pay Yourself First.

AUTOMATIC MILLIONAIRE ACTION STEPS

Reviewing the steps we laid out in this chapter, here's what you should be doing right now to get rid of your credit card debt . . . automatically.

❑ Stop carrying credit cards.

❑ Renegotiate your interest rates.

❑ Consolidate your debt—or if that's not possible, start DOLPing your credit card accounts.

❑ Decide to devote half the money you Pay Yourself First to paying off your balance.

❑ Make It Automatic by arranging for your credit card company to debit that amount from your checking account each month.

We're almost done. There's just one more chapter to go, and it covers something many people who want to be millionaires don't think about but should: how to get rich by giving back—specifically, how to make the world a better place by automating your charitable contributions and tithing.

FREE! MY GIFT TO YOU

In *The Finish Rich Workbook,* I wrote a detailed chapter on credit card debt. It covers how to get out of debt, how to fix your credit rating if you have a problem, and where to go for help if you need it. It also includes sample letters you can write to the credit card companies to get them to correct your credit record and outlines what legal protections are available to keep collection agencies from harassing you. If you feel you need more help in this area I'd like to offer you this chapter for FREE. You'll find it posted on my web site at www.finishrich.com. Enjoy.

CHAPTER EIGHT

MAKE A DIFFERENCE WITH AUTOMATIC TITHING

"We make a living by what we earn—we make a life by what we give."

—*Winston Churchill*

Having bought this book and read it all the way through to the final chapter makes you very special. Many people buy books about money, but few ever actually finish them. So congratulations. I hope you have been inspired to take some simple actions that will have a dramatic impact on your life over the long term.

The principles you've learned over the course of reading

this book are tried-and-true strategies for building wealth and financial security automatically. They are timeless. Put them into action and you will reach your financial dreams. But don't just focus on the result. You deserve to enjoy the journey.

Becoming an Automatic Millionaire is not simply about accumulating wealth. It's also about relieving stress and worries about the future—about putting yourself in a place that enables you to enjoy life now as well as in the future. In other words, having an automatic plan should not only change your future, it should also change your present.

With this in mind, I'd like to share one last step in our journey together—one that enables you to feel like a millionaire right away, even though it may be years before you actually become one. How can you do this? By being a giver as well as a saver—specifically, by using the tools that will enable you to become an Automatic Millionaire to make the world a better place.

THERE IS MORE TO LIFE THAN MONEY

The idea that there is more to life than money may strike you as a strange thing to read in a book about how to become a millionaire. But it's true. And deep down we all know this.

Now, don't get me wrong. Money is good, and I sincerely hope you get the riches you want. As the saying goes, I've seen rich and I've seen poor, and rich is better. But money will not give your life meaning. It really won't.

Why is it that we pursue wealth? I think we do it not for the things money can bring us (as nice as they may be) but in order to achieve a feeling. We may believe we want a nice car, a million-dollar bank account, a large home, money for retirement or our children's education, but ultimately what we really want is the *feeling* these things inspire in us.

Well, here is something to think about. As far away from your financial goals as you may think you are right now, you are much closer to achieving that feeling than you realize. In fact, even though you probably won't become a millionaire for years, it's entirely possible you could start experiencing that feeling in the next few weeks.

Would you like to know how?

HAVING IT ALL . . . THROUGH TITHING

What I'm about to share with you is a system that has been around nearly as long as civilization. It's called tithing.

What exactly is tithing?

Tithing is the proactive practice of giving back. It is a spiritual principle common to many traditions that says you should give back a portion of what you receive, that those blessed with abundance have a duty to help others through gifts of kindness, time, ideas, and money. What is amazing about tithing is that when you tithe you get a feeling we often associate with acquiring material things. You simply feel great.

We think more money and more stuff will make us feel

great, but this isn't always the case. Haven't you ever really wanted something, only to get it and wind up a few days later, the excitement gone, feeling strangely empty and disappointed? With tithing, the more you give, the better you feel.

YOU'VE PROBABLY HEARD OF THIS

Chances are that you're familiar with the concept of tithing. More than likely, the first time you heard about it was in a religious context, in your church, temple, or mosque. The word is based on the old Anglo Saxon word for "tenth," and the original idea was that you were supposed to donate to charity 10 percent of what you harvested from the land each year. But there is more to tithing than percentages and agricultural productivity. Tithing is not about following tradition or trying to rid yourself of guilt or hoping for some future reward. What it's really about is giving for the sheer joy of giving.

But here's something amazing. Although you should give simply for the sake of giving, the reality is that abundance tends to flow back to those who give. **The more you give, the more comes back to you.** It is the flow of abundance that brings us more joy, more love, more wealth, and more meaning in our lives. Generally speaking, **the more you give, the wealthier you feel.** And it's not just a feeling. As strange as it may seem, the truth is that money often flows faster to those who give. Why? Because givers attract abundance into their lives rather than scarcity.

AMERICANS ARE A VERY
GENEROUS PEOPLE

As a people, Americans are incredibly giving. In 2004, we donated roughly $250 billion in charitable contributions. And more than three quarters of that was given by individuals. Indeed, nine out of ten American households contribute to one or more charitable organizations. Moreover, approximately 93 million adults do some sort of volunteer work, with the average volunteer donating more than four hours of his or her time each week.

That's a pretty impressive record. And what makes it all the more impressive is the fact that, by definition, all this effort is unforced—the result of nothing more than the desire of people to make the world a better place. Sure, the government gives tax breaks to people who donate money to qualified charities, and being known as a philanthropist can improve your public image. But when it comes down to it, most giving is genuine.

HOW TO TITHE

Should you tithe? Ultimately, it's a personal decision. Still, I'd like to suggest that if you are not doing it now, give it a try. Take a percentage of your income and start donating it to some worthy cause. You could donate the 10 percent traditionally associated with tithing, you could donate more, or you could donate less. As I said, tithing is personal; it's not about percentages but about the love of giving. What's important is simply that you get started.

You might want to start small—say, by giving only 1 percent if your income—and let your contributions grow over time, just the way I suggested you start with Pay Yourself First. Not only will the process of starting create a momentum in your life that will change your destiny, but you will also be helping others in the process.

If this sounds at all attractive to you, take a look at the simple Five-Step Plan for Tithing that follows. If you are in a relationship, discuss it with your partner. See if it feels right. If it does, give it a try. You will be amazed how much doing things for others can do for you.

STEP ONE **COMMIT TO TITHING**

For tithing to work, it needs to be a consistent commitment. It's just the same as Pay Yourself First. If you donate a set percentage of your income every time you get paid, you will compile an impressive record of contributions. If you wait until the end of the year to see what is "left over," then you will wind up donating less—maybe even nothing.

Obviously, now that you've paid off your credit card balances, I'm not suggesting that you go back into debt in order to be able to tithe. Select a percentage that feels right to you and that you know you can manage. Once you've done that, make a commitment in writing to donating this amount on an ongoing basis.

THE TITHING COMMITMENT

Starting on _____ [insert date], I will
tithe to charity _____% of whatever I earn.

Signed: _____

STEP TWO **NOW MAKE IT AUTOMATIC**

Whatever amount you decide to tithe, arrange to have it automatically transferred out of your checking account on a regular basis. These days, doing this is easier than ever. Most organized charities will be happy to help you arrange an automatic transfer schedule (where they automatically debit your checking account on a regular basis), and many are set up to do it online in just a few minutes. If you are not comfortable having your bank account debited by a charity, you can probably set up an automatic transfer through your bank's online bill payment system. Most banks offer this service; simply call yours and ask.

STEP THREE **RESEARCH THE CHARITY BEFORE YOU GIVE**

Where you donate your money is entirely up to you. The most important advice I can offer is to make sure that the charity to which you are giving your hard-earned dollars really uses the funds it collects to help the people or causes it is supposed to be helping. Keep in mind that charity is a big business, and that administrative costs can eat up a huge percentage of charitable contributions. As a result, there are many charities that wind up spending most of what they take in not on the people they are supposed to be helping but on their own salaries and office overhead.

Not too long ago, I got very involved in a cause that was important to me. I donated a week of my time and raised nearly $20,000 in cash contributions—only to discover later that less than 40 percent of what they got actually went to the cause. While this money was still a huge help, I was disappointed that a higher percentage didn't reach the promised recipients. Now, virtually no charity can pass through 100 percent of what it raises. But they can certainly do better than 40 percent. Experts recommend looking for charitable organizations that pass through at least 75 percent of what they raise and staying away from those that pass through less than 50 percent due to high administration, management, and fund-raising costs.

So be a smart giver. Before you give, do some research and ask some questions. Here is a list of organizations that can help you learn more about potential recipients.

WWW.JUSTGIVE.ORG

This user-friendly web site is a great place to start, providing links to and information about a large number of organizations and causes you may want to consider supporting.

WWW.GIVE.ORG

This is the web site of the BBB Wise Giving Alliance, a nonprofit information clearinghouse formed in 2001 as a result of a merger of the National Charities Information Bureau and the Council of Better Business Bureaus Foundation and its Philanthropic Advisory Service. The alliance collects and distributes information on hundreds of nonprofit organizations that solicit nationally or have national or international program services. Before you make any donations, you should definitely see what they have to say about an organization you're thinking of contributing to.

WWW.GUIDESTAR.ORG

Formed in 1994, Guidestar aims to make charitable giving easy by doing the kind of due diligence responsible philanthropists know they should do but don't always have time for. Its web site is loaded with solid and helpful data.

WWW.IRS.GOV

Before you donate money to any organization, you should make sure it is recognized by the IRS as a bona fide tax-exempt charity under section 501(c)(3) of the tax code. To do this, visit the IRS web site and request publication #526 *(Charitable Contributions),* which covers in great detail what you need to know about charitable giving and documenting donations for tax purposes. You can also call the IRS toll-free at 800-829-3676 to request that they mail it to you.

STEP FOUR KEEP TRACK OF YOUR DEDUCTIBLE CONTRIBUTIONS

To encourage Americans to give more, the U.S. government has long allowed taxpayers to deduct contributions to qualified charities. Depending on how much you give, you can offset as much as 50 percent of your income in this way.

Of course, just because an organization calls itself a charity, that doesn't mean the IRS will let you deduct contributions to it. In order for a donation to be deductible, the organization must formally apply for and be granted tax-exempt status under section 501(c)(3) of the tax code. As noted above, you can verify this for any particular organization by visiting the IRS web site.

For contributions of less than $250, the IRS requires you to keep some sort of written record, such as a canceled check, a letter or receipt from the recipient, or a bank or credit card statement that verifies the where and when of the donation. If you give more than $250, the IRS wants your proof of donation filed with your tax returns.

You should be aware that not all charitable donations are 100 percent deductible. Say you spend $500 on tickets to a charity event where you play in a golf tournament or attend a gala dinner. Because you've received a benefit in return for your contribution, only a portion of your donation will deductible. The charity should be able to tell you how much of your contribution you can actually deduct.

STEP FIVE **FIND OUT ABOUT DONOR ADVISED MUTUAL FUNDS**

In recent years, a new type of mutual fund investment has appeared on the scene designed specifically for charity-minded investors. Called donor advised or charity funds, they allow people to invest their money for a charity's benefit later but get a tax deduction now.

These funds offer a number of benefits. Among them:

- **Instant tax deduction.** Once your money is deposited into one of these funds, you can take a tax deduction based on your IRS limits that same year—even though the money may not actually go to a charity until some later date.

- **More money for charities.** One of the neat things about these funds is the tax advantages they offer to people who want to donate securities that have substantially appreciated in value. Say, for instance, you bought a stock or mutual fund whose price subsequently soared. Instead of selling it, paying a hefty capital gains tax, and then donating whatever was left over, you can simply deposit the stock into a charity fund. While you take your tax deduction immediately, the investment can continue to grow tax-free until you direct the fund to cut a check to a selected charity—a check that is bound to be much larger than what the charity would have received after a straight sale.

- **Less pressure.** These funds are great for people who

know they want to give (and would like the resulting tax deduction now) but don't yet know whom they want to give to. You simply put whatever amount you want in the fund, take the deduction, and then make up your mind at your leisure about what the right charity is for you.

- **Creation of a legacy.** As your wealth grows (and it will because of what you are doing), you will increasingly be in a position to make a lasting difference in the world. Donor funds allow you to build a real charitable base for your family, since more than one person can contribute to the fund.

It's important to understand that once you invest in one of these funds, you've made an irrevocable gift. You can't get it back. The money has to stay in the fund until you direct the fund to give it to a charity.

Here are three established donor funds worth considering. As of this writing, the minimum initial investment in each is $10,000, with follow-up contributions starting at $250. Hopefully, as time goes by, the minimums on these funds will be lowered so that more people can use them.

Fidelity Charitable Gift Fund
1-800-682-4438
www.charitablegift.org

Schwab Fund for Charitable Giving
1-800-746-6216
www.schwabcharitable.org

The T. Rowe Price Program for Charitable Giving
1-800-564-1597
www.programforgiving.org

SOME OF THE WORLD'S WEALTHIEST PEOPLE TITHED BEFORE THEY BECAME RICH

If you study the lives of the great leaders, visionaries, and business people of our time, you will find a surprisingly common thread linking many of them: Long before they made their fortunes, they started tithing.

A great example of this pattern is Sir John Templeton. Arguably one of the world's greatest investors and a billionaire many times over, Templeton is recognized today as much for his philanthropic deeds as for his investment savvy. But Sir John didn't wait until he became rich to start tithing. He was a giver from the beginning—even when he could barely afford to make his rent.

Back in the days when Templeton and his wife were earning only fifty dollars a week, they Paid Themselves First 50 percent of their income—and yet they still managed to tithe. And he became a billionaire.

Hmm . . . something to think about?

AUTOMATIC MILLIONAIRE ACTION STEPS

Reviewing the steps we've laid out in this chapter, here's what you might consider doing to become an automatic tither.

❏ Decide how much of your income you want to give to charity.

❏ Pick a charity you care about, trust, and have researched.

❏ Automate your charitable donations on a monthly or biweekly basis.

❏ Keep track of your donations for tax purposes.

YOUR JOURNEY BEGINS TODAY!

If it's so easy to become an Automatic Millionaire, why don't more people do it? The answer is human nature: Most people simply don't do the things they know they should do.

Most people want to do well financially, but they never find the time or the energy to set themselves up for success. They hear about a program like this, but they invent reasons to ignore it. It sounds too easy to be true, they say. *Become an Automatic Millionaire? Yeah, right!* Or, worse, they buy a book like this one and get all excited about it, but don't do anything with their new knowledge.

Don't be one of these people. Keep in mind that you have

already done something incredible and you are now ready to change your future forever. You've taken action to buy and read this book. It's possible you've already begun acting on the ideas you've learned about handling money to Pay Yourself First and Make It Automatic. If so, great! If you haven't yet begun, now is the time to start.

Don't wait. The Automatic Millionaire program is based on simple principles that work. They are not difficult to implement. **You just need to start.**

Go back and reread whichever chapter inspired you the most. Maybe like me, you found that the story of the McIntyres touched a nerve, leaving you feeling, "If they can do it, so can I." (You would be right, by the way, to believe this.)

Maybe you're curious about figuring out your Latte Factor. I know from hearing from so many readers of my previous books that this simple little concept has changed thousands of lives. Can it change yours? The fastest way to find out is go back to page 50 and track your expenses for one day. See what happens when you do this, and see how motivated you become to Pay Yourself First.

Maybe you really loved the idea of muscling your way in line ahead of the government and Paying Yourself First. So why wait? Tomorrow, sign up for a retirement account at work or open up an IRA at a bank or brokerage. And **Make It Automatic,** so there's nothing further you need to do to keep the money rolling in. Remember—when you make your savings program automatic, you don't need discipline and you don't need time. You'll be Paying Yourself First AUTOMATICALLY.

Maybe you were struck by how much less worry there'd be in your life if you had a rainy day account that funded itself automatically. No matter what your circumstances, it's so much easier to enjoy life when you know you have several months' worth of expenses in the bank. If that sounds attractive to you, use the steps in Chapter Five to become one of those rare people who actually has a financial cushion to fall back on in case of emergency.

Maybe you are a renter who was encouraged by Chapter Six to become a homeowner. The fact is, you can't really become an Automatic Millionaire if you don't own your own home. And now you know how to become a debt-free homeowner automatically!

Maybe you're deep in debt and were motivated to adopt the automatic debt-free lifestyle described in Chapter Seven. It really can help you . . . if you take action.

Or maybe you were inspired by the idea of giving back. After all, wealth is not simply a matter of money; it's about a way of life. The more you share, the more you get back. Err on the side of giving more than you think you can give, and just watch how much abundance flows back to you.

In the end, whichever part of the Automatic Millionaire program appealed most to you, there is one question you should focus on: Why not? Why not apply what you learned in this book? Why not automate everything financial in your life? If you don't like the results, you can always go back to whatever system you were using beforehand.

Of course, my guess is that you won't want to go back. My guess is that once you set the Automatic Millionaire process in motion, you'll be happy to let it keep doing its thing while you get on with your life, no longer stressed about money or financial security. Before you know it, your future will be brighter. Instead of worrying about money, you'll be on your way to becoming an Automatic Millionaire. Maybe you'll go a step further and teach your friends to be Automatic Millionaires so they can take this journey with you.

Imagine your life five years from now with money in the bank, no debt, a home of your own, and a plan in place that will enable you to become rich and give back something to help others. Imagine if those you really loved were on the same journey. How great would that feel!

As you follow in the steps of Jim and Sue McIntyre and all the other Automatic Millionaires it has been my good fortune to meet, I want you to know that my thoughts and prayers will be with you. I know you are a very special person with unique dreams and gifts. I know you deserve to see them come true. I know you can do it.

If this book has touched you, I'd love to hear from you. Please share your success, challenges, and inspirations by e-mailing them to me at success@finishrich.com. Until we meet again, enjoy your life and enjoy the journey. Make it a great one.

AUTOMATIC MILLIONAIRE SUCCESS STORIES

Congratulations! By now, you are on your way to becoming an Automatic Millionaire. Or perhaps you skipped ahead and are reading this chapter first? Either way, I can't wait to share what's here. Since 2003, when *The Automatic Millionaire* was published, we've received thousands of e-mails and letters from people who have read the book and been inspired to make real changes in their financial lives. Was it easy for them? Read their stories and find out. As you read, I hope you will feel in your gut, *If they can do it, I can do it.* Because it's true! Maybe you can even do more!

I hope these stories of real-life success will inspire you to take action in your own life. Please let me know what happens. It is stories like yours that inspire me to do what I do. I would love nothing more than to include your story in a future book. To share your story with us, log on to www.finishrich.com or go right to www.finishrich.com/success.

Dear David,

The Automatic Millionaire caught my eye in a bookstore last July, while I was shopping with my family. I read a few chapters while they browsed and everything just made so much sense. I went home and put it on hold at the library, but in the end was unable to wait and purchased it.

When I look at the results, I am proud. Since July, I have started an emergency fund that has $1,800 and gets automatic deposits of $50 a week. I have increased my 401(k) contribution from 4% to 15%, and my husband's from 5% to 15%. I have set up almost every bill on automatic payment, and pay extra towards my home equity loan.

I am really proud of the fact that I talked 3 of my coworkers into signing up for the 401(k). The company has been giving away free money for years, but they never got around to signing up.

I really admire people who become successful without sacrificing their values. You have helped countless people, David, and I wanted to write and say thank you.

Kim Wright
Phoenix, AZ

Dear David,

I read *The Automatic Millionaire* twice after seeing you on *Oprah* and have started applying the principles to my finances. I have found out how to curb the "high maintenance woman" inside by approaching items that I purchase more methodically, rather than emotionally.

I am 48 years old and not working outside of the home. My husband, 44, is our sole breadwinner. I decided to Pay Myself First and started with $1,500 per month *plus* 30% of my husband's salary. (His company doesn't offer a 401(k), so the monies taken were after tax.) *In about six months' time, I was able to save over $30,000!* And because of that savings, I was able to help out my mom, who is terminally ill with lung cancer, to pay some of her medical bills, and ward off literally being forced to "sell the farm." In addition, we have been able to put the maximum allowed into our IRAs for the year 2005, and we have no credit card debt. We have no payments, other than our mortgage.

I am so pleased to find *The Automatic Millionaire* and *Start Late, Finish Rich* books written in an easy-to-read-and-understand format. *By applying these principles to our finances, I feel the magic of peace of mind, knowing that I am doing all I can to retire rich.*
Anna Hoffman
Deer River, MN

Dear David,
You're the best thing that ever happened to me! My life has been consumed by credit card debt for almost six years. I was divorced in 1999 and became a single mother on an income of $35,000. I agreed to a settlement that saddled me with $40,000 in credit card debt and a car loan of $8,000, just to avoid further legal fees. Everyone told me to file bankruptcy, but I'm happy to say that I didn't. And very proud, too.

Well, when I saw you on *Oprah* I stopped in my tracks. The folks you had on the show with you made me finally feel like I wasn't the only one in debt. I drove to the store and bought *The Automatic Millionaire.* I only put it down to sleep a few hours that night. I finished it the next day. I felt so refreshed. I just knew I could do this. It was so easy to understand.

I set up my Latte Factor sheet for the week, I set up a DOLP schedule and I called and lowered my interest rates, too. For once I felt good about working toward my goal of no credit card debt and I went at it with enthusiasm. I won! *As of June 29, 2005, I officially made my last credit card payment and was thrilled to call the company and close my account. I cut the card up into as many pieces as I could and was dancing around crying in pure joy!* It seemed like it took an eternity, but I did it! Yeah! I felt like I lost a hundred pounds.

I'm also proud to say that I've set up an account with ING Direct, which I never heard of until I read your book, and am saving automatically a little each week from my paycheck. And I have opened my 401(k) at work and was putting in 7%, but we got a raise last week of 3%, so I increased it to 10%! I love it!

David, you've given me gifts I never knew I could have. I've accomplished a huge goal, and once again found happiness, control over my life, power in myself, and determination. Being a single mom with those great characteristics will only help my daughter to achieve much in her life, too. So, you've touched us both.

Thanks again and God Bless you!

Theresa K.
Long Branch, NJ

Dear David,

Reading your book, *The Automatic Millionaire,* has changed my financial future. I have read many other personal-finance books but none of them motivated me to actually start planning for the future.

I immediately opened a money market account for an emergency fund (which we didn't have before). We opened IRAs and contributed the maximum. We increased my husband's 401(k) contributions to the maximum, and we're overpaying our house payment by $1,000 a month!

Even though I'm a stay-at-home mom, I feel like I have contributed so much to our retirement because before I read your book we weren't doing any of these things. I have such peace of mind that we're on the right track. I'm confident that we'll be millionaires by the age of 50.

I rave about your book to all of my friends and family and have bought your book for some of my friends. I was so excited to see that you wrote *Start Late, Finish Rich.* I've already bought it for my mom and she loves it!

Amanda Salgado
Cotesville, PA

Dear David,

We're feeling GREAT today after reading *The Automatic Millionaire.* Despite having three special needs children and the mounting bills that accompany them, we started the automatic deduction process ten years ago with my husband's 401(k). You really do not miss what you cannot see. *That automatic deduction has grown from zero to over $126,000* even though we have had to tweak our percentage to match our financial needs at any given time. Despite dropping to 2% some years, we are back to 18%.

I work two part-time jobs. I have $250 a week automatically put into a money market account to cover our Roth IRA contributions. I have $1,200 a month automatically withdrawn to be divided into 529 accounts for my two sons. We automatically put the rest of my pay into our emergency fund, which is over $20,000—five months' worth! Another $50 a week automatically goes into a vacation club. We also make one extra payment a year on our mortgage.

I am now in the process of having money from my second job put into either a SEP IRA or the new one-person 401(k). *Like you said, the only true way to do this is through automation. For years, we were very disciplined but could not commit. Now, we are used to it.* We live comfortably below our means knowing our future will be set! Not bad for a family beset with many challenges.

Marie Louise Kier
Chester Springs, PA

Dear David,

I recently finished reading your book *The Automatic Millionaire*. I just wanted to say thanks for inspiring my wife and me to take immediate action on saving and planning for our future. I need to give my wife the credit for buying me the book as well. As we're only 25 and 26 years old, *I believe we're well on our way to retiring like the McIntyres in the book.*

Real briefly . . . We saved up and bought our first house in November 2002 and have been proud homeowners ever since. I started my 401(k) at work over a year ago as well and now have a good $7,000+ in that, and my wife recently started hers. I have also recently increased my contribution from 5% to 8%. Everything we do is automatic.

With the amount of equity we raised in our house, we took out a home equity loan and paid off all of our credit card debt, high-interest car loans and store cards—saving us so much money each month. We have closed these accounts and have promised to just say no when it comes to opening any more of these accounts. If we don't have cash to buy it, then we obviously don't need it right away.

We also set up a savings account where we pay ourselves currently $75 a week. This cash we are determined not to touch. We also have a savings account with our bank as our emergency/backup savings if times go bad . . . and have close to two months' expenses saved. Unfortunately our mortgage lender does not have biweekly payments; however, I took your advice and have added an additional 10% to each payment.

So we're doing things as outlined in your book and will eventually increase our portions to our 401(k) as we learn to live with less. We've also been giving back by donating a small dollar amount of each check to charities of our choice. My wife and I just wanted to say thank you for inspiring us and we hope to one day be like the McIntyres and retire sooner than later.

Rick and Ann Longstreet
Hamilton, NJ

Dear David,

After attempting the Latte Factor for three days in a row, I realized that I don't really spend unnecessary money on the day-to-day expenses. I don't drink coffee; I've taken my lunch to work for probably the past ten years. What I figured out is that when I am in the grocery store or clothes shopping, I pick up all these extras that are not necessary. *I took my receipts from a past month and found over $600 worth of things I really didn't need or would not have missed had I not bought them.* This has allowed me to open an ING account and increase my 401(k), and pay more toward my debt.

Reading your book energized me to set my goals and see a clearer future, and I don't feel as stressed about my finances as I did. I may take a while to get to my goal, but I will not give up until I'm there.
Renee Frawley
Rowlett, TX

Dear David,

I must tell you, I don't read books, but I have not been able to put down *The Automatic Millionaire.* I found my Latte Factor; it is lottery tickets. I spend $9 twice a week. That's $72 a month and $864 a year, and I've been doing this over 10 years—at least $8,640. And how much have I won back? Probably under $200.

I have been saving money, too. About two and a half years ago I signed up for my 403(b) at work. I contribute 15% of every paycheck, and my company puts in 3%. I have $24,000 saved so far, and I also have $100 taken out of each paycheck for a savings bond. *I thought it was going to be hard, but I honestly haven't missed the money, and I know if I had the money I would have spent it.*

I am going to take this weekend to see if I have any more Latte Factors. My husband does, and boy, are we going to have a talk! This has been an inspiration! Thank you!
Diane Jodzio-Willson
Longmont, CO

Dear David,

I saw you on television a few weeks ago and immediately bought your book. I bought a second home three years ago and because of your book, I switched to a biweekly mortgage automatic payment system this week that will shave off seven years of payments and save me over $100,000. Thank you for your wonderful advice.

Bruce Miller
Austin, TX

Dear David,

I just wanted to take a minute to tell you how much I enjoyed your book, *The Automatic Millionaire.* I have never been interested in finance, investing, saving, or planning for retirement. In fact, I thought those who took an interest in money matters were self in-dulgent, stingy, and shallow.

However, my 50th birthday (!) is only a few years away, so "re-tirement" started to really enter my awareness. I saw you on the *Today* show and thought *The Automatic Millionaire* sounded so easy that maybe even I could do it. A few weeks later I saw the book and purchased it. It was an informative and easy read . . . and surpris-ingly uplifting!

In a few short weeks, I've opened an ING Direct account with automatic payroll deductions, increased my employer-matched re-tirement fund payroll percentage, and made substantial headway in paying off my credit card debt (now at $1,200 and falling rapidly). *I'm excited to begin this adventure— thank you!*

Tom Mantoni
Eaton, PA

Dear David,

On behalf of me and my future wife, I wanted to thank you for making my life automatic. My father has been trying to teach me about money for years, but I always thought it was too complicated or that I didn't have the extra income to make a difference. Little did I know that it was so easy. I was a quarter of the way through *The Automatic Millionaire* when I was so moved by your "How many hours per day do you work for YOURSELF" formula that I literally got up, went to my computer, and cranked up my 401(k) contribution from 4% to 15%! At the same time I also set up an additional deduction to my savings account. My fiancée and I live the exact same lifestyle as we lived before. However, our lives are richer knowing that there will be a pot of gold waiting for us at retirement. We're also looking to buy our first home next year and it makes it so much easier knowing that the money is there waiting for us. *The Automatic Millionaire* should be mandatory reading for every high school and college student across the country. The information is too good to pass up and it sure as heck beats chemistry. From the bottom of my heart . . . thank you. You've changed my life.

Chris Kesler
Austin, TX

Dear David,
Thank you so much for writing *The Automatic Millionaire*. I bought it yesterday and could NOT put it down. I actually just finished it now and it was one of the most amazing things I have ever read in my life. My wife and I both make good salaries but always made excuses to spend money. As a CPA and Financial Planner, I have begged her to start saving money, but when it comes down to it, we BOTH make excuses not to do so.

We do own a home and contribute to 401(k) plans, so it's not a total nightmare—I just always knew we could do MUCH better than we do. *As of now, I KNOW it's time to start saving, and with your program it should be pretty easy.* I am making her read the book tonight because I know it has already changed my life in terms of how I look at our finances, and it can change hers, too!

Thank you very much for writing that book—I hope to make it recommended reading for all my financial planning clients, too. I will be suggesting it every time I meet with a client. Take care!
Patrick Price
Oakland, CA

Dear David,
Your books (*Smart Couples . . .* and *The Automatic Millionaire*) have forever changed my life. I can never go back to the way I was after reading them. *Thanks to your simple "why didn't I think of this before?" plan, my family will retire wealthy.* We are a young military family and are on our way with the strategy you lay out in simple black and white. Thank heavens I found you just in time.

I find myself so excited about the subject of finances that I volunteer to teach others at church about how to be "money smart" and I always bring your books with me as recommended reading. I tell all of my friends and family about what I have learned in the books and hope that they will someday become as excited as I am. The books also make a great gift!

Thank you a million times for teaching me how to be a millionaire when I retire. YOU ROCK!
Sonja Yearsley
Pasco, WA

Dear David,
My name is Kat, and I will be a senior at Mercy High School in Baltimore, Maryland. I will be taking Micro and Macro Economics courses this fall. Our summer reading for the class included your book, *The Automatic Millionaire.*

Out of the eight ridiculously boring books plus yours (which I don't count as boring) I have to read before the start of term, I chose to read your book first because, even at seventeen, I have a love affair with money that would make my boyfriend jealous. I finished your book today, and it is, without a doubt, the most worthwhile read of my life. The most basic and necessary aspects of living in a consumer society are never taught in school. *Most young people I know are intimidated by money because they are under the impression that it's too complicated.*

Thus they get stuck in the cycle of, as you say, living paycheck to paycheck. My parents have worked all their lives, but they are almost sixty and have just refinanced the house mortgage, extending their payments for another ten years. At the dinner table, I "educated" them about everything I was learning from your book, and my dad was so interested, he's next in line to read it.

This book really gave me a clear direction for my financial future. Hopefully by starting early I'll be an Automatic Millionaire. I'll get back to you on that in a couple of years. I want to be able to take care of my parents the way they cared for me, so that will be my incentive to be successful in your plan. So thank you for sharing your expertise with America; we desperately need honest and simple financial advice. I'm off to read *Smart Women Finish Rich* . . . after I read my eight other assignments, that is. However, I don't think those authors will be receiving any fan mail from me.

I look forward to retiring a millionaire!

Thanks again,
Kat Harrington
Baltimore, MD

YOUR JOURNEY
CAN CONTINUE!

I hope you enjoyed *The Automatic Millionaire*—and that you
are already taking action based on what you've learned.

One of the key lessons in this book is that you can't get rich
renting! You have to buy a home.

Aside from "paying yourself first" automatically, nothing is
as important to your financial health as buying a home. And
if you buy a few homes over the course of your lifetime—
trading up or holding on to them—you can become an Automatic Millionaire Homeowner.

Does it sound hard? It's not. To help you complete this
journey of building wealth through homeownership, I've
written a follow-up book to this one. It's called *The Automatic*

Millionaire Homeowner. No matter where you are in your journey—still renting, planning to buy soon, or already an owner—this book will show you what's next.

THE AUTOMATIC MILLIONAIRE HOMEOWNER— READ A FREE CHAPTER NOW

To get you started, I want to give you a sneak peek at the new book right now. Visit our web site at **www.finishrich.com** and download a chapter. The download is absolutely free— it's my gift to you.

In it, you'll learn about John and Lucy Martin, an amazing couple I met who created lifelong financial security for them-selves—*automatically* through homeownership.

Their story is much like that of Jim and Sue McIntyre. The Martins are ordinary people on an ordinary income who learned the power of homeownership—and used it to build up a multimillion-dollar nest egg that made it possible for them to retire in their fifties.

Their approach was really simple and mostly automatic— and so easy that you can do it, too!

So come read their story—and let me take you on a journey to becoming an Automatic Millionaire Homeowner. It's as simple as deciding today that you're ready to be rich.

If you enjoyed this book, I know you'll love *The Automatic Millionaire Homeowner.*

Live Rich,
David Bach

ACKNOWLEDGMENTS

It takes many, many people to bring a book to life, and there are many, many people who have helped me along this journey to help others live and finish rich. *Smart Women Finish Rich, Smart Couples Finish Rich, The Finish Rich Workbook,* and now *The Automatic Millionaire* could never have reached the millions of people they have if I didn't have a team that supported and loved me. It is only because of the following people that I've been privileged to take this incredible journey around the world and reach so many with my ideas and writing.

To the following, I say a heartfelt THANK YOU!

First, to my readers: Over the past five years I've received thousands of letters and e-mails from you that inspire me to keep doing more of what I do. Your questions—as well as your stories of how my books have helped you take better control of your lives financially and go for your dreams—are what motivate me. To know I've touched so many of you makes all the writing, speaking, and traveling I do so worthwhile. I truly hope that this book meets your expectations and answers the question you've asked me over and over again: What's the REAL SECRET to finishing rich?

To my team at the Doubleday Broadway Publishing Group: This is a true partnership that I enjoy and appreciate. To Stephen Rubin, my publisher, and Michael Palgon, Bill Thomas, and Gerald Howard, thank you for your support of the Automatic Millionaire vision. This book is more than a book; it is a movement, and you are helping that movement take hold inside Broadway. To Kris Puopolo, my editor, this book was a true collaboration. You are the champion every author dreams of one day having. To Beth Haymaker, thank you for all of your support behind the scenes. You did a great job keeping us on track. To my PR team at Broadway, David Drake, Jessica Silcox, and Laura Pillar, this now makes four books! What can I say except that I deeply appreciate all you have done to help me get the message out. You have been believers since day one, and it is because of your guidance that we've been able to reach so many. To Catherine Pollock and Janelle Moburg, thank you for your marketing and sales efforts; you have both gone the extra mile on this book and its mission. To Jean Traina and John Fontana, thank you for the wonderful job you did on the cover; you've captured the spirit of this book beautifully.

To Allan Mayer, we've now worked on four books together. Few relationships in the world of writing last this long, and ours keeps getting better. Thank you; it's been a rewarding journey. And thank you for hanging tough through all the rewrites with a brand-new baby. This one is dedicated to baby Sasha and Renee!

To Jan Miller, my rock-star literary agent, I salute you. You took me on when I was just a financial advisor with a dream—and now look at us. A million books later, we've really started to do it! This is even more fun than I imagined. To Shannon Miser Marvin and Kim Wilson, you two are the best. Thanks for keeping track of everything that goes into doing what will be six books by 2006. I know I've worked you hard, and I really appreciate your dedication.

To my dream team that supports me at FinishRich, Inc., I owe so many thanks. First to Liz Dougherty, my "right hand." I was really blessed to have found you. Thanks for keeping my life together. You are a world-class strategic assistant. To my attorney, Stephen Breimer, I am grateful every day that I met you. Thank you for being such a wonderful sounding board—and protector—on every deal I do. To my team of agents, Mark and Erik Stroman of Entertainment Marketing Partners and Mark Pearlman, thank you for your vision, your insight, and your commitment to helping me reach more people. I'm excited about our future together. To my financial service agent, Harry Cornelius, we've now done deals for five years and counting. What a journey, and what a blast. You've been a true professional since day one.

Sometimes when you have a dream, you're lucky enough to find a partner who can help you make your dream a reality. For me, one of those partners has been Van Kampen Investments. We've worked together since 2000 to educate hundreds of thousands of people throughout North America with Smart Women Finish Rich and Smart Couples Finish Rich seminars. A very special thanks goes out to Dave Swanson, Scott West, Lisa Kueng, Gary DeMoss, Kristan Mulley, David Litton, Carl Mayfield, Jim Yount, Mark McClure, Eric Hargens, and Mike Tobin, along with the more than eighty wholesalers who have supported and taught the seminars thousands of times. To Jack Zimmerman, Dominick Martellaro, and Frank Mueller, thank you for your years of support. My deepest gratitude also goes to the thousands of financial advisors who now teach the FinishRich seminars each year. We've reached close to 500,000 people in the last four years. Truly amazing. To Morgan Stanley's Jack Kemp and Paula Dooher, thank you for sending me around the country to spread the message of *Smart Couples Finish Rich*. It was by far the most successful seminar tour I've done to date, reaching thousands of couples in a matter of weeks. I can't wait to tour again with you in 2004.

To the team at AOL—Tina Sharkey, Jodi Hooper, Jennie Baird, and Jamie Hammond—thank you for seeing instantly the power of *The Automatic Millionaire*. We are going to change many lives together. I'm excited to be the first America Online Money Coach. It's going to be an adventure.

Then there are my many mentors and coaches who continue to share with me. To Dan and Babs Sullivan, thank you for Strategic Coach, and thank you for teaching me how to take my knowledge and share it with the world. To Richard Carlson, Barbara DeAngelis, Tony Robbins, Mark Victor Hansen, Robert Allen, Robert Kiyosaki, Louis Barajas, Dottie Waters, Joe Polish, Bill Bachrach, Marcia Weider, Steven Krein, and so many more—each of you has taken time over the years to teach me personally how to get better at what I do, and for that I thank you again.

To my dearest friends in the world who continue to love me regardless of how long it takes me to return a phone call or e-mail, thank you for always being there for me. A special hug goes to Bill and Jenny Holt, Andrew and Belinda Donner, Betsey and T. G. Fraser, Jeff and Caroline Guenther, Jeff and Donna Odiorne, David Kronick, Bill and Courtney Decker, Michael Karr, and to our new dearest friends in New York, Steven and Rebecca Krein and Mary and Brant Cryder, thanks for making our new home feel like a home. Also, to the new dream team of entrepreneurs I hang with in New York—my YEO Forum (Roark, Asha, Tiso, Matt, "B"Martin, David, Tina, Eric)—I love you all! To my in-laws, Joan and Bill Karr, I was super lucky not only to find Michelle but also to be welcomed into a family where there is so much love and support. To my Nana and Grandma Goldsmith, I love you both so much; thanks for living a long life so I could learn from you.

To my parents, Marty and Bobbi Bach, who continue to be my biggest fans, I realize more and more every day how lucky I was to be your son. I deeply admire you as people and deeply love you as parents. To my little sister, Emily, and her husband, Tom Moglia, aside from how much I love you both, I am really, really grateful for the wonderful job you did taking over my financial planning business. The Bach Group was a large machine built over the course of a decade, and I know you've done an amazing job with our clients during the last few difficult years.

To my amazing wife, Michelle: over the last eighteen months, during which we moved to New York City, leaving behind our friends and family, I wrote three books, traveled a couple hundred thousand miles, and did a few hundred television and radio shows. And yet you still love me. Not only have you listened to me daily through good and bad, your feedback on this book made it what it is. To say thanks seems so small . . . but THANK YOU. We've now shared almost a decade of friendship and love, and each day I feel luckier and luckier to have found you. And to my unborn son, Jack, who as I write this is growing in his mother's womb, thank you for making me realize how special life is. Knowing you are on the way into our lives—that's really what it means to live rich. I can't wait to meet you.

Finally, to the thousands of people with whom I've met individually as a financial advisor, your life stories gave me a lifetime of lessons to teach others, and I now truly realize what a great gift that is.

I am profoundly grateful and love all of you!

David Bach
New York, 2003

INDEX

ABOUT THE AUTHOR

David Bach is helping the world learn how to live and finish rich and continues to inspire millions every day to take action to change their lives. He is the author of six consecutive national bestsellers including the #1 *New York Times* business bestseller *Start Late, Finish Rich,* and *The Automatic Millionaire,* as well as the national and international bestsellers *Smart Women Finish Rich*; *Smart Couples Finish Rich*; *The Finish Rich Workbook*; and *The Automatic Millionaire Workbook.* Bach carries the unique distinction of having had four of his books appear simultaneously on the *Wall Street Journal, BusinessWeek,* and *USA Today* bestseller lists. In addition, four of Bach's books were named to *USA Today*'s Best Sellers of the Year list for 2004.

Bach is also the author of *1001 Financial Words You Need to Know: The Ultimate Guide to the Language of Business and Finance,* published by Oxford University Press. In all, his FinishRich books have been published in more than 15 languages, with more than three million copies in print worldwide.

Regularly featured on television and radio as well as in newspapers and magazines, Bach has appeared twice on *The Oprah Winfrey Show* to share his strategies for living and finishing rich with the world. He has been a regular contributor to CNN's *American Morning* and has appeared frequently on ABC's *The View,* NBC's *Today* and *Weekend Today* shows, CBS's *Early Show,* Fox News Channel's *The O'Reilly Factor,*

CNBC's *Power Lunch,* CNNfn, MSNBC, and *The Big Idea with Donny Deutsch.* He has been profiled in numerous major publications, including the *New York Times, BusinessWeek, USA Today, People, Reader's Digest, Time, Financial Times,* the *Washington Post,* the *Wall Street Journal,* the *Los Angeles Times,* the *San Francisco Chronicle, Working Woman, Glamour, Redbook,* and *Family Circle.* He is a featured contributor to Yahoo! Finance, where his column, *The Automatic Millionaire,* appears biweekly.

David Bach is the creator of the FinishRich® seminar series, which highlights his quick and easy-to-follow financial strategies. In just the last few years, more than half a million people have attended his Smart Women Finish Rich® and Smart Couples Finish Rich® seminars, which have been taught throughout North America by thousands of financial advisors in more than 2,000 cities. Each month, through these seminars, men and women learn first hand how to take financial action to live a life in line with their values.

A renowned financial speaker, he regularly presents seminars for and delivers keynote addresses to the world's leading financial service firms, Fortune 500 companies, universities, and national conferences. He is the founder and Chairman of FinishRich Media, a company dedicated to revolutionizing the way people learn about money. Prior to founding FinishRich Media, he was a senior vice president of Morgan Stanley and a partner of The Bach Group, which during his tenure (1993 to 2001) managed more than half a billion dollars for individual investors.

David Bach lives with his wife, Michelle, and son, Jack, in New York, where he is currently working on his ninth book, *Start Young, Finish Rich.* Please visit his web site at www.finishrich.com.

Finishing Rich Is as Easy as 1-2-3! at finishrich.com

Step 1 Head to our web site at www.finishrich.com. There you can join our FinishRich Community by registering for my powerful FREE FinishRich Newsletter. Each month I'll send you my thoughts on the economy as well as useful ideas to help you succeed both personally and financially.

Step 2 Attend a FinishRich Live Event in your area. Each month, courses based on my books are taught throughout North America and 95% of them are FREE. Find the updated listings at www.finishrich.com.

Step 3 Download the FREE *Automatic Millionaire Jumpstart* audio. As our special gift for reading *The Automatic Millionaire,* I've created this highly motivational audio to get you to follow through on what you've learned.

How to Reach Us

Visit the web site at www.finishrich.com to get in touch. To share your success story, go to www.finishrich.com/success. I love hearing about your successes and I learn from your suggestions and questions. I promise—if you send it we will read it!

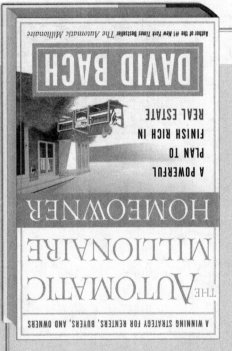

The Automatic Millionaire
Home Study Course

In this home study audio program packed with how-to tips, David takes a personal approach to the insights he shared in *The Automatic Millionaire*. You'll be coached by David as though he's in your home, car, or office as he reveals even more strategies, secrets, and tactics to help you turn an ordinary income into a lifetime of financial freedom...easily and automatically. The complete Automatic Millionaire Home Study Course is filled with critical tools and additional information you won't find anywhere else, including:

- ✓ 8 extraordinary audio sessions
- ✓ An Exclusive Bonus Session: How to Put Your Financial House in Order
- ✓ Accompanying Workbook on CD-ROM

Best of all, with The Automatic Millionaire Home Study Course, you'll have David Bach as your personal, one-on-one financial coach. Through these audio sessions, he'll be available to you whenever you need him, so you'll never forget your focus or lose momentum. You can check in anytime you want a strategy review, a shot of power, or a fresh dose of inspiration. And you can listen anywhere—while you're commuting, traveling—or even exercising!

Also included in the Automatic Millionaire Home Study Course is a copy of the #1 Bestseller, *The Automatic Millionaire*, and our exclusive Latte Factor Travel Mug.